AF700088

PARENTAL HANDBOOK

PARENTAL HANDBOOK

For Parents Dedicated to Local Control of Public Education of Children According to the Constitution

Adapted from

LIBERATE PUBLIC SCHOOLS
and
BUSING–NOT INTEGRATION–OPPOSED

Elmer Enstrom, Jr.
Public Interest Lawyer

The material quoted on pages 47-49 is
excerpted with permission from *The United States Law Week*,
Vol. 60, No. 15, pp. 3280-3281 (Oct. 15, 1991).
Copyright © 1991 by The Bureau of National Affairs, Inc.
(800-372-1033) <http://www.bna.com>

Please visit the Enstrom Foundation website at:
<http://www.enstrom-foundation.org>

Library of Congress Control Number: 2002090235
ISBN 1-882824-23-7

Copyright © 2002 by Elmer Enstrom, Jr.

First printing April, 2002

Printed and bound in the United States of America

Additional copies of this book may be obtained by sending US$10.00
($7.50 plus $2.50 shipping and handling) to:

Graphic PUBLISHERS
Post Office Box 10787
Santa Ana, California 92711-0787 USA
714.532.4379 Fax 714.532.4389
Toll-free orders: call 1.800.496.8726
jmillet@sbcglobal.net

California residents add 7.5% state sales tax

FOREWORD

On March 31, 1992 parents in San Diego and many other parents with children in public schools under court supervision in "desegregation" class actions welcomed the Supreme Court decision in **Freeman v. Pitts**. For it held that court supervision derived in such actions over student assignments be returned to the control of local authorities "at the earliest practicable date."

To many parents, this meant the return to local control of the education of their children and would allow them to participate regarding student assignment and other decision-making to fit local needs, as called for in the 1991 high court decision in **Board of Ed. of Oklahoma City v. Dowell**.

Many parents in San Diego had long opposed racial assignments of their children, sought since 1967 in **Carlin v. Board of Education**, a "desegregation" class action. As their *pro bono* counsel from May 12, 1979 until the case ended in 1998, I had continuously presented their opposition to racial balancing in that case, and their support for a return of local control so they could have a meaningful voice in the assignments of their children.

Their group, called "Groundswell," together with individual San Diego parents and children, intervened in the **Carlin** case on December 15, 1980. As their counsel, I raised two major objections to racial student assignments in a school district in which there never had been a finding of *de jure* segregation.

First, that such assignments racially discriminated against such non-consenting students and their parents, in violation of the California Constitution which applied federal decisional law requiring a finding of intentional segregation; and of the Civil Rights Act of 1964 in a district receiving federal funds.

Second, that continuing judicial authority governing such assignments infringed upon the constitutional right of the Groundswell Intervenors "to the governing participation to which they are entitled" in the operation of the District.

On September 10, 1981 the Los Angeles Superior Court terminated jurisdiction over the Los Angeles Unified School District to end litigation in **Crawford v. Board of Education**, which had occured before and after the 1976 California Supreme Court ruling in that case known as **Crawford I**. On September 15, 1981, the San Diego Board moved, as did the Groundswell Intervenors a day later, to end court jurisdiction in **Carlin**, but both motions were denied.

On May 21, 1985 the **Carlin** Court issued a "Final Order," which included a provision that "assignment to particular seats and to particular classes solely because of race and for the sake of the District's integration plans, as challenged in these proceedings, does not violate the constitutional rights of any of the children involved." The order also retained the San Diego District under court jurisdiction; and on May 4, 1989 the order was continued in effect without specifying a termination date, upon stipulation of the **Carlin** Plaintiffs and the Defendant Board, over Groundswell Intervenors' objections.

With the Board joining in that stipulation, it appeared my representation, which could have ended in 1981, would have to continue indefinitely until some way could be found to restore local control to the voices of the non-class parents. I willingly assumed this professional responsibility for parents otherwise unable to be separately represented. As rightly said, "*pro bono* service is a hallmark of the legal profession." Also, as a parent I felt parents' voices must be heard to advance the education of their children, as by emphasizing their needs instead of race in school assignments and by enhancing their ability to attend their neighborhood schools.

My own children from 1954 to 1968 had gone through the school system in San Diego in neighborhood schools which were later designated as "minority-isolated" in the **Carlin** case. As their parent, I witnessed the seeds of that case being sown when the Lindsley Committee conducted a hearing in 1966 regarding racial imbalance at Lincoln High School from which my eldest child had graduated and gone on to college.

I defended the education students were receiving, in a so-called "segregated" school, in a September 18, 1977 Commentary in *The San Diego Union* titled "Busing, Not Integration, Opposed." In answer to an earlier article "Segregation Makes San Diego Two Cities" implying that opposition to busing was racist and was in opposition to integration, I stated:

> In support of this misconception, which obviously disregards the polls which show that a majority of all Americans favor volun-

> tary school integration, are arguments I do not find persuasive...
>
> Then, from some cited examples, he apparently concludes that educators and white Americans will combine to discriminate against black Americans and the urban poor and see that there is inequality in the quality of their instruction and the education funds available to them.
>
> A somewhat similar charge was made concrning Lincoln High School in San Diego before the Lindsley Committee in 1966. At that time I defended the quality of the instruction my son had had at that high school and pointed out that a higher percentage of Lincoln High students had graduated from Harvey Mudd College (Clairemont [*sic*]) in 1965 than from any other high school.... Page 130 in Appendix I of *Liberate Public Schools*.

By coincidence, I too had graduated from my neighborhood school, Washington Junior High School, Pasadena, California, in 1931 with a large number of minority students, many of whom went on to college and successful careers.

Washington was in the Pasadena City School District, thereafter sued in state court by a black child to mandate it to allow him to transfer from Washington to another school he was unable to attend because of alleged racially gerrymandered school boundaries. The California Supreme Court, in **Jackson v. Pasadena City School District**, in 1963 reversed the lower court denial of a writ of mandate; and upon an issue presented only by two *amici curiae*, opined a duty upon school boards to take reasonably feasible steps to alleviate racial imbalance in schools "regardless of cause." *See* Note, 51 Cal.L.Review 810. This dictum became California constitutional doctrine in the 1976 **Crawford I** ruling, upon which the "remedy" in **Carlin** was based.

The Pasadena Board of Education was later sued in U.S. District Court and found in 1970 to have allowed illegally segregated schools to exist. In the following course of court supervision, the federal trial judge imposed a condition that "at least during my lifetime there would be no majority of any minority in any school in Pasadena." This condition, objected to by the Board as requiring annual reassignment of students, was struck down by the Supreme Court in 1976 in **Pasadena City Bd. of Educ. v. Spangler**. The lengthy Pasadena litigation is recited in **Spangler v. Pasadena City**

Bd. of Ed. (1979), which ended it.

The Pasadena example presents a due process flaw in desegregation class actions whereby students subject to such race-based assignments, and their parents, lack a separate voice in the proceedings. As the real parties in interest to a declaration subjecting such students to perpetual reassignment, they could have made a much stronger objection than that it "inconvenienced" their board.

It seemed to me that similarily onerous conditions were imposed upon the DeKalb County School System in the ruling by the Eleventh Circuit appealed by the DCSS in **Freeman v. Pitts**, which were:

> ...The DCSS must consider pairing and clustering of schools, drastic gerrymandering of school zones, and grade reorganization... The DCSS and the district court must consider busing regardless of whether plaintiffs support such a proposal. The DCSS's neighborhood plan is not inviolable... **Pitts by Pitts v. Freeman**.

These conditions affected not only the petitioner DCSS, but more directly the students who would be subject to reassignment on the basis of their race. Since the DeKalb students were not parties before the high court, I believed their interests should be separately presented by Groundswell Intervenors, as *amici curiae*. Accordingly, their *amici curiae* brief was filed in the **Freeman** case in support of the petition of DCSS.

Upon the favorable result in **Freeman** on March 31, 1992, Groundswell Intervenors filed a motion on April 6 in the **Carlin** case to terminate court jurisdiction. But the San Diego Board switched from its 1981 position, urging termination, to urging its continuance in opposition to the Groundswell motion and subsequent motions.

It took until July 1, 1998 for Groundswell Intervenors to end the **Carlin** case, over strong opposition by the **Carlin** Plaintiffs and Defendant Board, first before the trial court and then the appellate court. The extraordinary experience in restoring local control, under those circumstances, by ending a class action aimed at non-class persons is reported upon by me as their lawyer in the following two books.

The first book, published in 1998, *Busing—Not Integration—Opposed*, illustrates how the Constitution was invoked by Groundswell in opposition to the continuing effort by the Plaintiff-Class in the **Carlin** case to racially balance San Diego City Schools.

The Sequel, *Liberate Public Schools from Government by Lawsuit,* titles the solution sought by parents opposing continuing racial balancing of their children in **Carlin**-type lawsuits. The Sequel presents, chronologically, the constitutional opposition proffered in the **Carlin** class action to "desegregation" orders before-during-and-after imposition of them.

This Handbook adapts those books for parents dedicated to local control of public education, especially those long deprived of a meaningful voice in the school assignments of their children by reason of "desegregation" class actions versus their boards of education. The Handbook reports the challenges met by San Diego parents, in gaining legal representation, in intervening, and in asserting their constitutional rights in such a class action—**Carlin v. Board of Education**—over a period of 17-plus years. And, finally, they gained termination of the lawsuit over the opposition of both the **Carlin** Plaintiffs and Defendant Board.

Challenge One initiates the San Diego parental *amici curiae*, challenge to "busing," as real parties in interest, entitled to intervene in the **Carlin** class action versus their school board.

Challenge Two continues the San Diego parental challenge to "busing," as intervenors in **Carlin v. Board of Education**.

Challenge Three reflects the San Diego parental *amici curiae* support of the challenge in **Freeman v. Pitts** by school officials to a busing order, adversely affecting similarly situated parents, by an intermediate appellate court.

Challenge Four records the continuing San Diego parental challenge to "**Carlin**" court assignment of their children, toward restoring local control of their public schools.

Challenge Five relates the San Diego parental challenge to perpetual "**Carlin**" court assignment of pupils, to restore local control according to the Constitution.

Challenge Six asserts that other parents can likewise challenge court assignment of pupils similarly occurring in their school districts, to restore local control according to the Constitution.

The Handbook concludes with the means available for parental challenges toward restoring local control—particularly as to assignment of their children—in districts where it has long been absent because of "desegregation" class actions against school boards.

DEDICATION

To my wife, Klea,
and to our children
James, Robert, Mary, and John
whose support enabled me
to become a lawyer

The Elmer Enstrom family, March, 1959.
San Diego Historical Society, Photograph Collection

INTRODUCTION

Comprehensive Anatomy of
Carlin v. Board of Education
A Thirty-Year California "Desegregation" Class Action
Superior Court of San Diego County, No. 303800

Kari Carlin, *et al*., Plaintiffs

v.

Board of Education, San Diego Unified School District

Defendant

Groundswell, *et al*., Intervenors

(See particularly events where Groundswell parents filed *amici curiae* briefs when faced with the **Dilemma** (direct) or (indirect) of court orders, sought of their board in the **Carlin** case, directly affecting them; or sought in other "desegregation" class actions versus boards of education which could indirectly affect them by *stare decisis* application of precedents. Events in this "anatomy" are detailed in *Liberate Public Schools from Government by Lawsuit* (LPS) at the pages noted.)

June 27, 1963

Jackson v. Pasadena City School Dist. 59 Cal.2d 876,881. Dictum: "(T)hat school boards take steps, insofar as reasonably feasible, to alleviate racial imbalance in schools regardless of its cause."

December 4, 1967

Plaintiffs, a group of students of diverse races, including "Caucasian," filed this action against the Defendant Board of Education to "Integrate the San Diego School System." The White enrollment was then 76 percent.

December 7, 1973

The Court determined the existence of a class action and described the class as "(a)ll students attending the San Diego Unified School District and their parents and legal guardians *who believe that said schools should be racially balanced, if necessary through court order.*" (Emphasis added)

June 28, 1976

Crawford v. Board of Education, 17 Cal.3d 280 (**Crawford I**). Transformed **Jackson** dictum into constitutional doctrine as to both *de jure* and *de facto* segregation in California schools.

March 10, 1977

After a hearing and determination (upon the complaint by the **Carlin**-Plaintiff-Class) that the Defendant School Board had "failed to take some reasonable steps to alleviate school segregation and the harms inflicted by such (*de facto*) segregation," the Court issued a Writ of Mandate commanding the Board—

(1) to present a "detailed plan to further alleviate racial segregation" in 23 named schools;
(2) to implement "some portion of the plan during the school year 1977-78 and to designate target dates for the operation of those portions of the plan, if any, that are to be implemented at a later date;" and
(3) to "serve and file a return to this Writ on or before June 13, 1977."

May 29, 1979

Groundswell's motion to intervene is denied, but *amici curiae* status granted Groundswell, *et al*. **Dilemma** (direct).

October 2, 1979

Judge declines to order forced busing for forthcoming school year, but **Carlin** Plaintiffs then propose an order for appointment of a special master with power to make mandatory pupil assignments.

October 10, 1979

Groundswell, *et al*., were granted permission to file brief as *Amici Curiae* and Interested Persons in opposition to the motion for appointment of a special master, and brief was filed (Appendix). **Dilemma** (direct). (Appointment was not made).

November 6, 1979

Proposition 1 amended California Constitution (Sec. 7(a), Art. 1) to apply federal decisional law to disallow judicial pupil school assignment or pupil transportation to racially balance school districts *not* found to have caused *de jure* segregation.

December 15, 1980

Groundswell, an association of persons, along with six District students and their parents, *intervened in opposition to court-ordered race balancing in the District schools*, in behalf of similarly situated students, parents, and citizen-taxpayers.

This opposition was presented formally at a hearing on July 16, 1981, and was reiterated throughout the pendency of the case. The White enrollment had declined to 55.4 percent.

December 19, 1980

Crawford v. Board of Education, 113 Cal.App.3d 633 (**Crawford II**), rendered, upholding the constitutionality of Proposition 1 which amended Section 7(a), Article I of the California Constitution.

September 10, 1981

Final Approval of School Board Desegregation Plan and Discharge of Writ of Mandate by Los Angeles Superior Court Judge Robert B. Lopez in **Crawford v. Board of Education**, No. 822854.

September 15, 1981

The Defendant Board, later joined by Groundswell Intervenors, moved to terminate all court proceedings, (based on the Los Angeles **Crawford** Superior Court precedent), which was opposed by the **Carlin** Plaintiffs, and later denied.

June 30, 1982

Crawford v. Board of Educ., etc., 458 U.S. 527 (**Crawford III**) affirmed **Crawford II**.

May 21, 1985

"Final" Order Re: Integration Plan (retaining jurisdiction).

May 4, 1989

"Final" Order Re: Integration Plan, as Amended May 1989 (continuing order retaining Court jurisdiction).

May 11, 1990

Groundswell Intervenors applied to the Supreme Court, and, with consent of the parties, filed an *amici curiae* brief in support of the petitioning Board of Education of Oklahoma City Public Schools, presenting views in behalf of Oklahoma City "counterparts" not directly before the Court. **Dilemma** (indirect). Oklahoma City school officials ultimately prevailed upon their petition for *certiorari* in **Board of Ed. of Oklahoma City v. Dowell**, *infra*. LPS at 48-52.

January 15, 1991
Board of Ed. of Oklahoma City v. Dowell, 498 U.S.237.

May 1, 1991
Groundswell Intervenors applied to the Supreme Court, and, with consent of the parties, filed an *amici curiae* brief in support of the petitioning DeKalb County School System, Georgia, presenting views in behalf of DeKalb County "counterparts" not directly before the Court. **Dilemma** (indirect). DCSS school officials ultimately prevailed upon their petition for *certiorari* in **Freeman v. Pitts**, *infra*. LPS at 52-56.

March 31, 1992
Freeman v. Pitts, 503 U.S. 467; 112 S.Ct. 1430.

April 6, 1992
Groundswell moved again to terminate all court jurisdiction, but the Board, speculating its ending might result in getting less state integration money, reversed positions and joined **Carlin** Plaintiffs in opposing Groundswell's motions, which were denied. (A Groundswell petition for extraordinary relief to the Court of Appeal was denied.)

April 1, 1994
Amendments to the Ralph M. Brown Act, intended to strengthen public participation in local government, became effective.

July 22, 1994
Groundswell moved a third time to terminate all court jurisdiction (based additionally upon Brown amendments), but motions were again opposed by Defendant Board and **Carlin** Plaintiffs and denied October 21, 1994.

October 28, 1994
Groundswell's Motion for Reconsideration of denial of motions to terminate proceedings filed.

April 11, 1995

Brief by State Senator Quentin L. Kopp, author of Ralph M. Brown Act amendments intended to strengthen public participation in local government, as *Amicus Curiae* and Interested Person, filed in support of Groundswell motions to terminate jurisdiction. It voices the interest of legislators. LPS at 63-65.

June 12, 1995

Missouri v. Jenkins, 515 U.S. 70; 115 S.Ct. 2033.

September 19, 1995

Motion by Marion Nixon, *et al.*, to Intervene (denied October 23, 1995; and Motion for Reconsideration denied December 15, 1995).

November 8, 1995

Brief by State Assemblyman Steve Baldwin, some constituents being within the Defendant Board's jurisdiction, as *Amicus Curiae* and Interested Person, filed in support of Groundswell motions to terminate court jurisdiction—voicing his interest. LPS at xiv.

December 15, 1995

Groundswell motions to terminate all court jurisdiction and discharge writ of mandate granted (formal order granting motions being filed January 12, 1996); Final Order Terminating Court Jurisdiction to be determined later.

July 26, 1996

Hearing held in which a "Final Order" is determined along the lines submitted by the Board and **Carlin** class, to continue court jurisdiction without providing for discharge of the writ of mandate.

August 21, 1996

"Final Order Terminating Court Jurisdiction" continuing court jurisdiction until at least January 1, 2000, filed. (A petition by the Groundswell Intervenors and Interested Legislators to the Court of Appeal for extraordinary relief from this order extending jurisdiction such a length without providing for discharge of the mandate was denied (remedy lay in appeal). Their petition for review to the California Supreme Court was denied.)

November 5, 1996

The electorate adopted the California Civil Rights Initiative (Proposition 209), which was upheld on April 8, 1997. **Coalition for Economic Equity v. Wilson**, 110 F.3d 1431 (9th Cir. 1997); reversed **Coalition for Economic Equity v. Wilson**, 946 F.Supp. 1480 (N.D.Cal. 1996).

August 21, 1997

The Ninth Circuit denied Coalition's request for a rehearing and/or rehearing *en banc*; and on August 26, 1997 denied **Coalition**'s request for a stay of issuance pending the filing and determination of a Petition for *Certiorari* with the United States Supreme Court.

August 22,1997

Upon a fourth motion by Groundswell, Court modified Final Order Terminating Court Jurisdiction to provide in an order filed September 5, 1997 for termination of Court jurisdiction on July 1, 1998 if Supreme Court had upheld Proposition 209 by then.

August 28, 1997

Proposition 209 took effect in California.

August 29, 1997

Coalition filed a Petition for Writ of *Certiorari* with the United States Supreme Court (**Coalition for Economic Equity, *et al.*, v. Wilson, *et al.***, U.S. Docket No. 97-369, 66 U.S.L.W. 3171 (1997)) and sought an immediate stay, which was denied on September 4, 1997.

October 21, 1997

Defendant Board filed Petition for Writ of Mandate to vacate portion of Order Modifying Final Order Terminating Court Jurisdiction, filed September 5, 1997, terminating Court jurisdiction on July 1, 1998, upon the upholding of Proposition 209 by the Supreme Court (which occurred on November 3, 1997). **Coalition for Economic Equity v. Wilson**, 139 L.Ed.2d 310 (Cert.Denied).

February 9, 1998

The Fourth District Court of Appeal denied Defendant Board's Petition for a Writ of Mandate to vacate portion of trial court's order terminating court jurisdiction on July 1, 1998, and continue jurisdiction to January 1, 2000 without providing for discharge of the March 10, 1977 writ of mandate. **Board of Education v. Superior Court**, 61 Cal.App.4th 411. LPS at 98-99.

July 1, 1998

The Trial Court discharged the 1977 Writ of Mandate pursuant to a motion by Groundswell, joined by Interested Legislators Kopp and Baldwin, over the objections of Board and **Carlin** Plaintiffs. The formal order (filed September 30, 1998) stated that the Final Order Terminating Court Jurisdiction, dated August 21, 1996, "remains viable" as no party appealed that Order. LPS at 99-101.

The White enrollment had declined still further, to 29 percent.

October 20, 1999

Following the Board's proposals (108) of modifications of its Integration Plan, the author presented written and oral objections (November 30, 1999) to the manner in which the race of the students was to be utilized in their school and classroom assignments in the Integration Plan. LPS at 108-111.

January 25, 2000

The Board adopted an Integration Plan which may require further modification in accord with the objections of the author, as high court rulings subject such affirmative action to strict scrutiny. LPS at 111-114,138-139. San Diegans can now directly voice to the Board objections to plans adversely affecting their children, with the restoration of local control.

TABLE OF CONTENTS

CHALLENGE ONE

SAN DIEGO PARENTS CHALLENGE BUSING OF THEIR CHILDREN, IN CARLIN V. BOARD OF EDUCATION, AS REAL PARTIES IN INTEREST, ENTITLED TO INTERVENE

Background

In June of 1977 thirty-five people met in their neighborhood area in San Diego in response to a notice by a fellow citizen that their children were faced with "some sort of mandatory busing assignment" arising from a "desegregation" class action filed in 1967 known as the **Carlin** case.

Parents had reason to be concerned, because their school board in a series of meetings seemed to be preparing them for the forced busing of their children away from their neighborhood schools. They were "staged" at various schools around the District in the manner as described to a news reporter by a citizen, who became President of the group of parents, calling themselves "Groundswell":

> ...The whole tenor of the meeting was—get ready because it's (busing) coming and there is nothing you can do about it. That was the way it was presented. Make whatever accommodations you have to but just accept it.

Instead of "just accepting it," the President and about 300 other members of Groundswell, from June to October 1977, gathered the signatures of about 22,300 persons in support of a "Neighborhood Schools Amendment" to the Constitution. It included a provision that "(n)o student shall be compelled to attend public school other than the one nearest his residence...." The petitions were submitted to their congressman, but the House of Representatives failed to act upon those and many additional petitions to so amend the Constitution.

Author, as a Parent, Publishes Concerns About Busing

In the meantime the author, whose children had gone to San Diego schools, had been watching the hearings in **Carlin v. Board of Education, San Diego Unified School District**, in which a class of students and their parents (**Carlin** Plaintiffs) asserted the racial balancing of San Diego schools, "if necessary through court order." The **Carlin** Plaintiffs, in hearings in early 1977, relied upon 1976 **Crawford I**, which went beyond federal rulings requiring a finding of *de jure* segregation, to hold that school boards had a duty to alleviate racial imbalance "regardless of cause."

The **Carlin** attorneys disturbingly demanded that this expansion of judicial power (that is, ordering students bused on a racial basis to correct "*de facto*" segregation) be applied in San Diego. Their tone is reflected by the following excerpts from their argument reported in *The San Diego Union* on January 25, 1977:

> (T)he "time for voluntary plans is over… they only postpone the inevitable…." (counsel for **Carlin** Class)
>
> (T)he court asked, "Do you think it is the duty of the district (to desegregate the schools) no matter what the price to individual children… the law must march on?
>
> "A difficult question, but yes, the law marches on…." (counsel for **Carlin** Class)

To the author, that approach mirrored other desegregation decrees which, to echo Supreme Court Justice Lewis Powell, placed a burden upon innocent children and their parents who were not charged with any offending action. That was the burden—compelling children to leave their neighborhood and spend significant time each day being transported to a distant school—resisted fiercly elsewhere. Also, litigation history taught that those decrees had derived from *stare decisis* application of rulings in cases in which their individual interests had not been separately represented.

The author concluded there was a necessity for a fuller articulation of constitutional objections to forced busing on behalf of innocent persons subject to it. Weren't these innocent parents and their children subject to such busing the real parties in interest? Weren't they being shut out of individual representation in these desegregation actions directed toward their school board members who, of course, were not so affected by the busing remedy sought? And wasn't the rarity of their separate appearances in the precedential and other actions, directed solely against school authorities, approving such a remedy, indicative of their financial inability to gain separate individual representation?

These concerns led to Enstrom's commentary to *The San Diego Union* on September 18, 1977, titled "Busing, Not Integration, Opposed." *See* Appendix I to *Liberate Public Schools*.

Groundswell Parents Achieve *Pro Bono* Representation

The Groundswell group learned of Enstrom's 1977 commentary, leading to a request early in 1979 that he represent them *pro bono* in the **Carlin** case. It then appeared that the **Carlin** Plaintiffs were dissatisfied with an all-voluntary integration plan instituted by the Board pursuant to the March 10, 1977 Mandate to alleviate *de facto* segregation, and would demand court-ordered busing at the annual July review of the plan.

The group having been unable to obtain counsel, Enstrom undertook the representation and on May 29, 1979 filed Groundswell's motion to intervene, which was denied on June 14 as untimely. But *amici* status was granted and, as such, on July 3, 1979 he briefly argued the point that objecting persons would be racially discriminated against by the proposed busing, citing Chief Justice Earl Warren's *Memoirs* (pp.287-8):

> "Again the Court was unanimous in its decision of May 31, 1955, reaffirming its earlier decision of May 17, 1954, by asserting the fundamental principle that any kind of racial discrimination in public education is unconstitutional, and that all provisions of federal, state, or local law requiring or permitting such discrimination must yield to this principle."

On October 2, 1979 the Court filed its Order Re: Integration Plan for the forthcoming school year without requiring mandatory pupil assignments. But the threat continued, for the plan would be reviewed yearly, and the **Carlin** Plaintiffs filed an appeal from the failure to include a busing segment in that order.

In the meantime, the California electorate had debated and then on

November 6, 1979 adopted an "anti-busing" amendment (Proposition 1) to the California Constitution limiting busing to that permitted under federal decisional law. But this amendment too faced appeal by the **Crawford** Plaintiff-Class whose ACLU-affiliated counsel were also co-counsel for the **Carlin** Plaintiffs.

Following the adoption of Proposition 1, the reformed Los Angeles Board moved to discontinue busing in that city, but the trial judge denied it on the grounds of an earlier judicial finding of *de jure* segregation by that district. A precursor of the strong effort which would be made to judicially overturn Proposition 1, approved by about 66% of the Californian electorate, came in a San Bernardino Superior Court desegregation action in which there had not been a finding of *de jure* segregation.

On January 3, 1980, the San Bernardino trial judge permitted the ACLU-affiliated attorneys to appear and argue orally "in support of the unconstitutionality" of Proposition 1 in behalf of the **Crawford** plaintiffs, as *Amici Curiae.* Following that, Enstrom submitted, but was denied permission to appear and argue, *amici* briefs, one by the Groundswell group alone first and then one joined by a statewide group, Californians Against Forced Busing. (Details in *Busing—Opposed*, Chapter 2).

This exclusionary ruling indicates how hard it has been for persons who would be adversely affected by a judicial decision of a legislative nature to be heard in the proceedings leading to that decision. Groundswell applicants felt their arguments were more to the point than those by the **Crawford** counsel who, as stated, were also co-counsel for the plaintiffs in the **Carlin** case (*id.*,ch.2). And later they were vindicated by the strong language by the Supreme Court in ultimately rejecting **Crawford** Class arguments in an effort to overturn Proposition 1 on appeal from **Crawford v. Board of Education**, 113 Cal.App. 633 (1981) (**Crawford II**). *See* **Crawford v. Board of Education**, 458 U.S. 527, 535-545 (June 29, 1982) (**Crawford III**), *also id.*,ch.2.

On May 19, 1980, the **Crawford** trial judge formally denied the efforts of the Los Angeles Board to stop the busing in Los Angeles, on the ground it was justified by a 1970 finding of *de jure* segregation. **Crawford v. Board of Education**, Superior Court No. C-822,854, p.3. Ultimately, on September 12, 1980, before Chief Justice (then-Justice) William Rehnquist, the L.A. Board failed to gain a stay of a California Supreme Court order which left standing the trial court order "requiring mandatory reassignment of between 80,000 and 100,000 first- through ninth-grade (Los Angeles) students attending approximately 165 elementary and junior high schools…." **Board of Ed., Etc. v. Superior Court**, 448 U.S. 1343. But Enstrom saw hope for Groundswell parents in the following concern expresed about bystanders by then-Justice Rehnquist, while being unable to grant a stay on the record before him (448 U.S. at 1347):

> "…Because projections indicated that the school district in 1987 will consist of only 14% white students, the Superior Court asserted its task was to achieve the optimal use of white students in the schools so that the maximum number of schools may be desegregated.
>
> "I find this analysis somewhat troublesome, since it puts 'white' students much in the position of textbooks, visual aids, and the like—an element that every good school should have. And it appears clear that this Court, sooner or later, will have to confront the issue of 'white flight' by whatever term it is denominated…."

This expression was in line with Enstrom's belief that the key to possible success of the non-Class Groundswell students and parents rested in separate representation by intervention. Thereupon, they could assert consideration as "persons" not "elements" in the case and present constitutional issues that school boards lacked ability to pose in these cases, but individuals could raise.

Grounds Build for Intervention by Groundswell Parents

Notwithstanding Proposition 1, on October 3, 1980 the **Carlin** Class applied for an order to appoint a Special Master who would design an integration plan to "maximize classroom integration in every school in the District." The Groundswell group requested, and was granted, leave to appear and file a brief, as Interested Persons (under Proposition 1) and *Amici Curiae*, in opposition to the **Carlin** Class application (which did not succeed). They alleged that it was unconstitutional to appoint such a Special Master, with power "to make mandatory pupil assignments on the basis of their race to particular schools" in the District.

This brief acclaimed the right of Groundswell parents to be heard separately and directly in this class action, as the real parties in interest, and set the tone for them to do so for the following seventeen years. For those interested in the contentions on behalf of non-class parents, who remain outside the loop of litigation in these class actions, it is set forth as the Appendix to this *Handbook*.

On October 21, 1980, the staff of the San Diego Board proposed a mandatory busing plan for the next largest school district in California. This action followed a September 8 memorandum by the **Carlin** judge questioning whether the voluntary plan was meeting the **Crawford I** requirements. The Groundswell persons, of course, were also facing the "busing" success of the **Carlin** Plaintiffs' ACLU-affiliated counsel in Los Angeles, and their continuing determination to press for busing in San Diego by overturning any limitation to it posed by Proposition 1. According, every legal effort, necessarily by intervention, must be made to prevent it.

Groundswell Parents Prepare for Intervenor Status

The first step, of course, was to prepare intervention pleadings in behalf of the association, Groundswell, and individual parents and their student children, and others similarly situated, versus the Board and **Carlin** Plaintiffs as defendants-in-intervention. Basically, Groundswell parents claimed that:

> "The mandatory assignment of student intervenors, and others similarly situated, because of their race, to particular public schools within said District violates, and would violate, the rights of Intervenors and others similarly situated....
>
> —under the California Constitution, including the Due Process and Equal Protection Article, for racial discrimination against both parent and student intervenors;
>
> —under the United States Constitution, including the Equal Protection Clause of the 14th Amendment, for state action racially discriminating against both parent and student intervenors; and the Due Process Clause of the 14th Amendment (a) for infringing upon the liberty of parent intervenors to guide the destiny of their children, and (b) for infringing upon the liberty and privacy of

student intervenors, by improper state action;

—under Title VI of the Civil Rights Act of 1964, for subjecting both parent and student intervenors to discrimination on the ground of race under a program and activity receiving federal financial assistance.

Groundswell Parents Meet First Challenge by Gaining Standing to Oppose Busing as Intervenors

On December 12, 1980, at a spirited hearing in a courtroom filled by Groundswell supporters, their motion to intervene was granted, over objections by both the **Carlin** Class and the Board, and was formalized December 15. The attendance at this hearing by the now-Intervenors was followed by their next exercising the right of petition under the First Amendment.

In furtherance of establishing their role in the case as "persons," separate petitions were prepared for those (1) students, (2) taxpayers-voters, and (3) taxpayers-parents, residing in the District who objected to the proposed mandatory student assignments as a violation of their respective rights. Those rights had been asserted in the intervening complaint as noted above, and the petitions were drafted to fit the category of the persons signing them, such as this one for students:

> "I, the undersigned student, residing in the San Diego Unified School District, respectfully object to school authorities making me, because of my race, go away from my neighborhood public school location to classes, without my consent and the consent of my parent(s), as a violation of my rights." *See* exemplar in *Busing—Opposed*, p.142.

District students signed 1,856 of the total of about 5,983 petitions presented by the Groundswell president to the Board on March 3, 1981, of which exemplars in each category were later made a part of the record in the **Carlin** case. *Id.*,app.V.

In the meantime, on December 22, 1980 (seven days after this intervention) the California Court of Appeal reversed the **Crawford** Superior Court, finding that that trial court's 1970 findings did not support the conclusion that the Los Angeles District had violated the Constitution through intentional segregation. It further concluded that Proposition 1 was constitutional under the 14th Amendment and that plaintiffs were not entitled to a greater remedy than was provided by the federal Constitution. **Crawford II**, *supra*.

The **Crawford** Plaintiffs unsuccessfully petitioned the California Supreme Court for review, and then petitioned the U.S. Supreme Court for a writ of *certiorari* to reverse **Crawford II**.

Carlin Plaintiffs' co-counsel thereby were making a strong effort to continue judicial authority to mandatorily bus students for racial balance without having to show their school board had caused the "segregation" to be so alleviated.

Groundswell Parents, as Intervenors, Prepare for Trial

Concurrently, there was no lessening of the effort by the local ACLU counsel to impose busing in San Diego by the **Carlin** Plaintiffs, who had appealed the lack of a busing segment in the present order.

In the preparation of this representation, Enstrom's objections to forced busing in his 1977 commentary were transformed into the manner in which they would be posed at the intervention trial. The pleadings, and then the evidence, would reflect that the opposition was founded upon a truism stated in 1620 when the colonists were first forming their first legislative assemblies:

> "Every man (and woman) will more willingly obey laws to which he (or she) hath yielded his (or her) consent."

It would be shown that persons facing judicial affirmative action affecting them without going through the democratic process left them with no recourse but to assert their objections in the court proceeding in which it was being imposed.

The history of desegregation litigation reflects the extension of **Brown v. Board of Education** in 1954 from discontinuing segregation in public schools; to **Green v. County School Board**, requiring affirmative "desegregation" in rural schools; and then to **Swann v. Charlotte-Mecklenburg Board of Eduation**, applying such affirmative action in urban schools found to have committed *de jure* segregation.

Crawford I in 1976 extended such affirmative action to California schools regardless of the cause of what was termed *de facto* segregation. The **Carlin** Plaintiffs sought to apply that ruling to the Groundswell parents who could now, as intervenors, present objections before busing affecting them could be ordered. Early Groundswell parental initiatives by petition and other lawful steps, set out in their *amici curiae* brief (*see* Appendix), established the special interest of non-class parents to orders adversely affecting their children in the **Carlin** class action.

CHALLENGE TWO

SAN DIEGO PARENTS CHALLENGE BUSING OF THEIR CHILDREN, IN CARLIN V. BOARD OF EDUCATION, AS INTERVENORS IN THIS CLASS ACTION

Groundswell Intervenors go to Trial

The foregoing litigation history was in mind in the preparation for the intervention hearing. The Intervenors established the intervening (1) parents and (2) students as "persons" in accordance with their complaint, by the following stipulation with the **Carlin** Plaintiffs and the Board:

> 1. That the parent intervenors were citizen-taxpayers residing in the District, and were continuously opposed to the "mandatory assignment of" their children "and others similarly situated because of their race," to particular schools within the school district, and to the use of tax monies for that purpose; and further that they are and would be substantially affected by such assignment.
>
> 2. That the student intervenors attended their neighborhood District schools, and were continuously opposed "to the mandatory assignment" of them "and others similarly situated and affected, because of their race," to particular public schools within the school district; and further that they are and would be substantially affected by such assignment.

On July 16, 1981, at the hearing, a stipulation of facts also established that San Diego public schools, administered by the Board as the governing agency, including those attended, and to be attended, by student intervenors, received federal funds.

Following the receipt in evidence of the stipulated facts, Enstrom stressed the legislative nature of the relief being sought in this desegregation case. He argued this presented a need for latitude to respond accordingly to "protect us from the request for mandatory assignment which will come in the Courts of Appeal, and the higher courts beyond that."

The Court took judicial notice of several cases upon which the **Carlin** Class relied for the judicial authority for busing, offered to show they had been decided by a course in which there was no separate representation of the interest now presented by Intervenors. A declaration by the Groundswell president, to which all counsel stipulated he would so testify, emphasized this point, first, by stating he had supported initiative Proposition 21 adopted November 7, 1972 which provided:

> No public student shall, because of his race, creed, or color, be assigned to or be required to attend a particular school.

Then, the following portions of his testimony showed how he had been left out of the process leading to the mandatory busing his children were facing:

> ...3. That upon the passage of Prop. 21, he was not aware of any proposals, law or court ruling which would mandate the assignment of his children, because of their race, to some school away from their nearest neighborhood school wherever they might choose to live; and had he known of such he would have exercised every right available to him as an elector and taxpayer in opposition thereto.
>
> 4. That his children, one of whom is an intervenor, continuously attended their neighborhood schools.
>
> 5. That he first learned in the spring of 1977 of activities arising in their schools from the **Carlin** case that his children might be subjected to forced busing.
>
> 6. That he also learned of the case of **Crawford I** and did not believe his interests and those of his children and others similarly situated were represented in the course of the proceedings leading to that decision...

Then the Groundswell president established the existence of individual opposition to the proposed busing by (1) taxpayers-parents, (2) students, and (3) taxpayers-voters by the presentation of their petitions (with about 5,983 signatories, of whom 1,856 were children) to the defendant Board, as follows:

> 11. On October 21, 1980, an elementary exchange program was proposed to the Board of Education of the SDUSD which I am informed and believe and therefore allege calls for forced busing of elementary school students in said district. Thereafter, I and about 40 other members of "Groundswell" circulated petitions among residents of the SDUSD in the following three categories: (1) taxpayers-parents, (2) students, and (3) taxpayers-voters.
>
> 12. On March 3, 1981, I presented to the SDUSD Board a number of petitions bearing approximately 5,983 signatures, including signatures in each of the above categories, with the attached memorandum of transmittal ("respectfully object(ing) to the mandatory assignment of children, because of their race, away from their neighborhood school location in the San Diego Unified School District....")

Having provided a foundation for the Intervenors as "persons" by the facts established in the declaration, their objections were offered as evidence the Court could consider in rejecting mandatory student assignments.

Excerpts from the Reporter's Transcript of Proceedings on July 16, 1981 follow:

> MR. ENSTROM (Counsel for Intervenors): ...The number of students signing those petitions was 1,856. And the original petitions have been filed with the School District.
>
> THE COURT: Will counsel stipulate, if called he (Mr. Lester) would so testify?
>
> MR. STERN (Counsel for SDUSD): Yes, your Honor.
>
> MRS. ROESER (Counsel for Plaintiffs): So stipulated.
>
> THE COURT: I don't think it will be necessary for Mr. Lester to testify, because they have stipulated if called he would so testify. The question before me really is the relevancy of any or all of these documents. And I would like to go through them with you and make rulings. No matter what my rulings are, you have made your record, which of course is vital to your interests....
>
> MR. ENSTROM: Very well. I offer Exhibit 1, the vote on...

the Wakefield Initiative, enacted November 7, 1972.... I want to put in the vote, to show the vote in San Diego County. I think it goes to the issue of white flight, along with the other evidence which shows this long, deep, and continuing opposition to mandatory assigments. Of course, we ultimately hope to argue the point made by Professors Berger, Kalodner, and others, that the Court should not be—to order mandatory busing is [a] violation of the separation-of-powers provisions of the State and Federal Constitutions....

THE COURT: The Court will sustain the objection....

MR. ENSTROM: Exhibit 3 is the vote on Proposition 1, the constitution[al] (*sic*) amendment [to] the California Constitution, enacted November 6, 1979.

THE COURT: Well, the objection again will be sustained on the grounds of irrelevance.... [Exhibit] Six is the declaration from Mr. Lester, which I have read.... And I will sustain the objection there, too, on the ground it is irrelevant....

MR. ENSTROM: But it is offered for a number of different purposes, your Honor.

THE COURT: If you wish to speak further to it, I of course will listen to you.

MR. ENSTROM: For instance, Paragraph 1, I seek to establish (h)is (*sic*) standing to raise these matters as a registered voter and taxpayer.

THE COURT: That was stipulated to, wasn't it? Isn't that part of your stipulation? I thought it was. That is my recollection. I don't think anyone questions it....

MR. ENSTROM: [Paragraph] Number 8 shows the gathering of these 22,000 signatures, which goes to the white-flight effort (*sic*). Evidence of white flight. That a person[s] (*sic*) would feel so strongly about this that they would gather that many signatures and present them to their congressman for such action as he could take. I think that is evidence bearing on that issue.

MRS. ROESER: If the Court is considering admitting those, I would like to speak to that and cite cases, of which there are many, showing those are not the type of considerations the Court may take into account.

THE COURT: I agree with you, Mrs. Roeser. I have no question in my mind that it is irrelevant. On the other hand, if it will possibly circumvent a technical problem on appeal to admit that many people did vote for it, it would seem to me….

MR. ENSTROM: Signed the petition.

THE COURT: …it would seem to me to be the more cautious way of approaching it. If you insist, I will sustain the objection. I would suggest, however, that the counsel stipulate whatever number there are, signed the petition. You can do as you please.

MRS. ROESER: I think we already stipulated that is what he would testify to. But we object to the admissibility.

THE COURT: That is true. Counsel stipulated that is what he would testify to. Although I sustained the objection to both the declaration and what he would testify to on the grounds of irrelevancy. The facts are there, and they are uncontradicted. And if, for instance the appellate court found that I have erred, and I should have entertained that evidence, then it is there.

MR. ENSTROM: Yes, your Honor. Of course, I am urging that in these cases where the Court assumes a legislative role, there is a great deal more latitude as to what your Honor is required to consider in all of these matters. In other words, certainly a legislative committee which would consider these matters….

THE COURT: Especially one that wanted to be returned to office.

MR. ENSTROM: My point is, where the Court assumes a legislative role, along with that goes greater latitude as to what evidence you want to receive.

THE COURT: You know, Mr. Enstrom, judges are never consistent. You know that. I sustain the objection.

MR. ENSTROM: [Paragraph] Number 12, the allegation of course is the presentation to the Board of these 5,900-plus signatures, which goes to show again this long, deep, and continuing opposition to the forced busing as it bears on white flight.

THE COURT: Just a moment. Yes, go ahead.

MR. ENSTROM: Number 12, that bears on white flight, particularly. When I refer to white flight, I am talking about the issues of objectors leaving the school system, which has been a matter about which evidence has been received. And I don't think it is necessarily referring to any particular race.

THE COURT: No... Still... I sustain the objection to the declaration....

THE COURT: Exhibit 8 you are referring to?

MR. ENSTROM: Exhibit 8, yes. I would like to have that received in evidence.

THE COURT: What is this all about?

MR. ENSTROM: That refers to the elementary exchange program. We want to show the staff introduced a forced busing program to the District on October 21. About a year after Proposition 1 was passed. It goes to the allegation in our complaint in intervention that the Board will be forced to consider from time to time plans involving the mandatory assignment of pupils. And it gives a history of that.

THE COURT: I don't see any harm in 8.

MRS. ROESER: No. your Honor.

MR. ENSTROM: It is part of the official record.

THE COURT: Congratulations. Eight is in evidence....

MR. ENSTROM: The last item was showing in Item 15 of the declaration that these members of Groundswell have discussed the necessity for representation of their interest. They have inquired of various attorneys as to the necessity and availability of representation; and throughout this entire period they are unable to pay attorney's fees.

THE COURT: Is that Number 9?

MR. ENSTROM: That is Number 15 in our declaration, your Honor. Item 15. We have nothing by way of an exhibit.

THE COURT: You just want to establish that fact?

MR. ENSTROM: That mainly goes to the due process.

THE COURT: The plaintiffs are impecunious—not impecunious, but are unable to pay for counsel?

MR. ENSTROM: We want to point out particularly, the real party (*sic*) in interest, particularly the minors in these cases, the children that are opposed to busing, are not financially able to come into these cases and be represented.

THE COURT: Very few people are.

MR. ENSTROM: And that the assumption of a legislative role by the Court denies these children of due process because they can't come in and be heard. They don't have the financial resources to do so.

THE COURT: Well, that is a form of argument which I don't—there is nothing before me to rule on.

MR. ENSTROM: I wanted that received in evidence, that portion of the declaration.

MRS. ROESER: Objection, your Honor. It is full of hearsay, among other things.

THE COURT: Well, I will sustain the objection. But I don't think you are harmed in any way, because I think it is a matter the Court can take judicial notice of, that most people cannot spend thousands and thousands of dollars for counsel to represent them in matters of this sort, or any sort as far as that goes. So I don't believe you are in any way harmed by my not accepting it. I would personally take judicial notice of that as a common fact. I will take judicial notice of it, that most people can't afford lawyers.

MR. ENSTROM: I think this is particularly hard on the youngsters, your Honor, who we contend are pawns—became pawns in this type of situation without representation, and this series [of] cases have shown that.

I will close by making two points, your Honor. That the District now has a plan which is non-discriminatory and voluntary. To introduce mandatory assignments would be to introduce discrimination into a voluntary non-discriminatory plan. And (*sic*) obvious government involvement in discrimination. I made that point in my brief. I would just reiterate, we have many, many children in the District who are opposed to the—to their being assigned away from their schools without their consent, or the consent of their parents. I do cite the Reitman case for the proposition that government—the government should not inject discrimination into the—to a voluntary non-discriminatory plan which would occur in the event of mandatory assignments, on account of the race of the children assigned.

> THE COURT: All right, sir. thank you very much. Thank you, Mr. Enstrom. And thank you for being patient. Thank your clients for being patient, also.
>
> MR. ENSTROM: Thank you.

On September 8, 1981, the **Carlin** Judge filed his Order Re: Integration Plan 1981-1982 without mandating reassignment of students. This was the distinguished trial judge's last act in this case, from which he resigned, to be followed by two similarly respected judges before it concluded.

Court Jurisdiction Ends in Los Angeles **Crawford** case, but continues in San Diego **Carlin** case

Earlier in 1981, following the denial of review of **Crawford II** by the California high court, the Los Angeles Board directed that mandatory student assignments be ended there. On April 20, 1981, approximately 7,000 pupils took the option to return to their neighborhood schools, of whom 4,300 were minority students. **Crawford III**, *supra*, 458 U.S. at 534, Fn.10. That board followed that action by efforts to end judicial jurisdiction over the Los Angeles District.

On September 10, 1981, the newly-presiding Los Angeles Superior Court judge terminated jurisdiction in the **Crawford** case by approval of a voluntary integration plan and discharge of the writ of mandate, with these words:

> ...Judicial intervention is no longer appropriate. The people, who are the ultimate authority, must look to the School Board, as their elected representatives, to continue to discharge its duty under the law.

Five days later on September 15, relying strongly upon the Los Angeles precedent, the San Diego Board moved to similarily terminate the **Carlin** case. The next day, on September 16, the Groundswell Intervenors also so moved, adding the grounds that it would restrain the **Carlin** Plaintiffs (1) from seeking court-ordered busing in violation of Proposition 1, and (2) from seeking to racially discriminate against Groundswell students by state-imposed busing in violation of the 14th Amendment.

Both the motions by the Defendant Board and Groundswell Intervenors were denied on December 12, 1981 by the newly assigned judge. Thus the San Diego district continued under court jurisdiction during the pendency of the appeal from **Crawford II** to the Supreme Court, which was upheld on June 29, 1982 by **Crawford III**, *supra*.

Groundswell Intervenors Meet Second Challenge of Recording Opposition to Busing, But **Carlin** Judge Continues Court Jurisdiction Over Student Assignment Indefinitely

On September 14, 1984 the **Carlin** judge issued his Memorandum of Intended Decision, which evolved into his Statement of Decision on May 21, 1985. The conclusion of this Statement, however, indicated the tone of the conduct of this strongly contested proceeding by commending each counsel for the three parties by name "for their very able representation of their clients and for their assistance to the Court as officers of the Court."

In the "Final" Order Re: Integration Plan, also filed May 21st, there was a paragraph which was first embodied in the September 14, 1984 memorandum, continuously challenged by Groundswell Intervenors:

> 1983-84 17. Assignment to particular seats and to particular classes solely because of race and for the sake of the District's integration plans, as challenged in these proceedings, does not violate the constitutional rights of any of the children involved.

Furthermore, the "Final" Order was not final in that Paragraph 11 contained this provision:

> After the entry of this Order the Court will retain continuing jurisdiction of this matter but will take further action only upon noticed motion for good cause shown.

The Board not only did not object to this extension of jurisdiction, but in reversal of its 1981 motion to terminate all court jurisdiction, embraced both that paragraph and Paragraph "1983-84 17." This change of position portended a need for a much longer *pro bono* representation than, for instance, was required by the Bustop attorneys because of the closure of the

Crawford proceedings in September, 1981. For, now the burden would be placed upon Intervenors to show cause for concluding jurisdiction, as will be seen, over the objections of both the **Carlin** Plaintiffs and the Board.

Board and Plaintiffs Stipulate to Continuing Court Jurisdiction

In March, 1989 the Board proposed a stipulation, containing the above two provisions, objected to by Groundswell on April 29, 1989, as follows:

> ...In addition, the proposed Amended Final Order extends and enlarges the jurisdiction of the Court over School District Affairs in a manner contrary to Intervenors' long-standing positions and, we believe, to the evolving Supreme Court view on affirmative action.
>
> In particular, Intervenors refer (1) to their support on September 16, 1981, of the District's motion to discharge the writ of mandate and (2) their objections to the following language in the Final Order re: Integration, filed May 21, 1985, which is restated on Page 12 in the proposed Amended Final Order, as follows: (restating Paragraph "1983-84 17" sanctioning racial balancing of classes and seats within classes).

Notwithstanding the objections, the stipulation by the other two parties was approved and the Amended Final Order re: Integration was signed and filed on May 4, 1989. The argument that the "evolving Supreme Court view on affirmative action" would support the objections was bolstered by indications that the high court would soon review orders which mandated busing in Oklahoma City and DeKalb County, Georgia.

The Groundswell parents had met the challenge of voicing their objections to busing before the **Carlin** Court. The author undertook to place parents' special opposition to busing indirectly before the justices by way of *amici curiae* briefs. The first brief, after garnering consents from the parties, was served and thereupon filed on May 11, 1990 in support of the successful petitioning achool board in **Board of Ed. of Oklahoma City v. Dowell**, 498 U.S. 237 (1990). Details concerning this brief are reported in *Liberate Public Schools*, pp. 48-52, and in *Busing—Not Integration—Opposed*, pp. 51-58.

The author next served and filed on May 1, 1991, the second *amici* brief of Groundswell Intervenors to the Supreme Court, in support of the petitioning DeKalb County school officials in **Freeman v. Pitts**, 503 U.S. 467 (1992). The Groundswell parents, as did countless other similarly situated parents, eagerly received the decision in that case as leading to a return of local control over school assignments of their children.

CHALLENGE THREE

GROUNDSWELL INTERVENORS SUPPORT CHALLENGE TO BUSING ORDER, IN FREEMAN V. PITTS, A CLASS ACTION, TO RESTORE LOCAL CONTROL OF STUDENT ASSIGNMENT

On March 31, 1992 many parents in the DeKalb County School System, Georgia (DCSS), welcomed the decision in **Freeman v. Pitts**, allowing for the first time since 1969 citizens in that school district to run their own schools as to assignments of their children.

They had apparently overcome the challenges facing parents trying to have their school boards seek the end of continuous judicial sanctioning of the racial school assignments of their children in "desegregation" class actions. This is because school assignments sought in these class actions impact upon them rather than upon the board members, who are sued and must consider other interests in determining their actions.

Fortunately the interests of those in DeKalb County targeted for busing were represented when the DSCC board successfully opposed an appellate order for the indefinite busing of their children. But the difficulty that school board had in attaining the end of court supervision challenges parents to obtain ways to do so more fairly and speedily, as noted by Justice Scalia:

> ...(W)e must resolve—if not today, then soon—what is to be done in the vast majority of other districts, where, though our cases continue to profess that judicial oversight of school operations is a temporary expedient, democratic processes remain suspended, with no prospect of restoration, 38 years after **Brown v. Board of Education**... **Freeman v. Pitts**, *supra*, 112 S.Ct.1430,1450.

Appeal to Supreme Court by the DeKalb County School System Illustrates Extraordinary Difficulty in Restoring Local Control

The record in the **Freeman** case reflects the difficulty of the DCSS in establishing "a finding that no portion of the current racial imbalance (was) a remnant of prior *de jure* discrimination" before restoration of complete local control.

The DeKalb County School System (DCSS) in Georgia had been operating under the direction of the district court since June 12, 1969 in a school desegregation case brought earlier by a black plaintiff class. At that time the trial court, among other things, enjoined the defendant DCSS from discriminating on the basis of race, and ordered the DCSS to close all remaining *de jure* black schools and to establish a neighborhood school attendance policy. **Pitts by Pitts v Freeman** (11th Cir. 1989), 887 F.2d 1438,1443.

DCSS then "closed all *de jure* black schools," and, it appears from the litigation history related in the panel decision, established a neighborhood school attendance policy, and a "M to M program." The latter program permitted students to transfer from schools in which their race is a majority to schools in which their race is a minority, which was modified in 1976 to provide those students with free transportation. *Id.* at 1443.

The history relates a series of requests by the parties and orders leading to the reversal in 1985 in "**Pitts I**, 775 F.2d 1423" by the 11th Circuit of a district court conclusion that DCSS had achieved unitary status. *Id.* at 1443. More litigation followed leading to a June 30, 1988, district court decision, from which both parties appealed. *Id.* at 1444.

The plaintiffs contended to the appellate court panel, among other things, that the "district court erroneously dismissed the DCSS from court supervision in the area of student assignment." Oppositely, the DCSS contended, among other things, that it "satisfied its duties relating to student assignment when it complied with the district court's 1969 order and closed all *de jure* black schools." The DCSS took "the position that it did not 'cause' resegregation and that it possesse(d) no duty to take affirmative action to desegregate." *Id.* at 1444.

The record reflected that demographic changes had affected the DCSS since 1969 and had resulted in racial imbalance in which the percentage of blacks in the district increased dramatically since then until the time of the ruling by the district court. *Id.* 1441-42.

Nevertheless the Eleventh Circuit Panel reversed the district court's conclusion that the DCSS fulfilled its duties in the area of student assignment and, in its reversal, stated:

> ...The DCSS must consider pairing and clustering of schools, drastic gerrymandering, and grade reorganization... The DCSS and the district court must consider busing—regardless of whether plaintiffs support such a proposal. The DCSS's plan is not inviolable.... **Pitts by Pitts**, *supra*, 887 F.2d at 1450.

The Circuit Panel then ordered that the district court require the DCSS to prepare and file a plan in accordance with its opinion in the shortest reasonable time. *Ibid.*

The Supreme Court granted a petition for *certiorari* by the DCSS to hear its appeal from this order, and heard the arguments of the parties on October 15, 1991. Their arguments were reported in *The United States Law Week*, headnoted by that report's statement of the ruling being appealed. Pertinent excerpts from that report, at 60 LW 3279, at 3280-81, follow:

> The Eleventh Circuit ruled that DCSS will not receive unitary status "until it maintains at least three years of racial equality in (the six **Green**) categories, student assignment, faculty, staff, transportation, extra-curricular activities, and facilities." Furthermore, the court said, "DCSS must consider pairing and clustering of schools, drastic gerrymandering of school zones, and grade reorganization." After 20 years of court supervision, the Eleventh Circuit concluded, "DCSS continues to operate racially identifiable schools. The DCSS has never achieved unitary status and it retains the duty to eliminate all vestiges of the dual system."
>
> ...Rex E. Lee, of Provo, Utah, argued before the Supreme Court on behalf of DCSS. According to Lee, DeKalb County grew rapidly after the issuance of the 1969 order to desegregate. Since that time, he said, the percentage of black students in the school population increased from 5 to 50 percent. And, he continued, the district court concluded it was the shift in population that caused the resegregation, not any action taken by DCSS....

The approach Lee urged upon the court was for it to look at what caused the segregation in question. If you do that, he said, **Pasadena**… disposes of both issues in this case. First, he said, the demographic shifts are not attributable to DCSS, and thus should not reflect upon its unitary status. Second, the non-attainment of one factor in **Pasadena** did not require an overall change in the other factors.

Lee shifted gears and closed with a discussion of federalism and the efficient allocation of resources. Under **Dowell**, he said, school systems should be run by local governing bodies, and not federal courts. For 22 years, DCSS has been trying to obey the law, but now, due to circumstances beyond its control, it is being told it will have to continue under court supervision for an indefinite length of time. Under the Eleventh Circuit's opinion, Lee noted, his clients are looking to more busing and radical gerry-mandering….

Christopher A. Hanson, of New York, argued on behalf of the black student plaintiffs. In his opening remarks, he noted that the county was purposely segregated even after **Brown**, that, as the district court found, the system was never fully desegregated, and that the schools today are both separate and unequal with fewer resources being spent on black students.

What if all the **Green** factors are satisfied Stevens asked, but a student imbalance remains?

It is the duty of the board, Hanson answered, to break the pattern of segregation….

In response to a question by Stevens dealing with the difficulty DCSS may have desegregating at this point, Hanson said that if the job is harder today, "that's the board's fault." Had the board followed the mandate of **Brown** or the decrees when they were handed down, the system would already be desegregated and there would be no problem….

In rebuttal, Lee said it is easy to suggest what should have been done in the past. But, he continued, the district court said nothing would have worked. Furthermore, nothing in the court of appeals' opinion indicates anything could have been done by the board. This case is not fact specific, Lee said, it's legal. The students have

> conceded that after the black schools were closed the system was desegregated, and thus this case should go back to the district court so DSCC can prove that its faculty assignments meet the requirements of the plan.

On March 31, 1992, the Supreme Court reversed the judgment of the Court of Appeals overruling the district court's conclusion that DCSS had fulfilled its duties in the area of student assignment, and could relinquish supervision in that area as headnoted. (**Freeman v. Pitts**, 503 U.S. 467):

> The Supreme Court, Justice Kennedy, held that district court has authority to relinquish supervision and control over school district in incremental stages before full compliance has been achieved in every area of school operation.

Groundswell Intervenors File *Amici Curiae* Brief Supporting DeKalb County School System Petition To Uphold District Court's End of Judicial Supervision Over Student Assignment

As noted earlier, an *Amici Curiae* brief was filed in support of the petitioners **Freeman**, *et al.* (DCSS), by the Groundswell Intervenors. They alleged "a strong interest in seeing that a busing order based what is at most *de facto* 'segregation' is not issued, which could be used as a precedent elsewhere to racially reassign voiceless students after they have been able to attend their neighborhood schools for years."

This unique brief derived from the concern of Groundswell Intervenors toward the Eleventh Circuit's reversal of a "district court's conclusion that the DCSS had fulfilled its duty in the area of student assignment...." The Eleventh Circuit then ordered the district judge to "require the DCSS to prepare and file a plan in accordance with (its) opinion with the shortest reasonable time." 887 F.2d at 1450.

As previously noted, the Circuit opinion included this provision:

> ...The DCSS and the district court must consider busing—regardless of whether plaintiffs support such a proposal. The DCSS's neighborhood plan is not inviolable.... *Id.* at 1450.

The Groundswell *Amici* argued its presentation was appropriate:

> The affirmative relief ordered by the panel adversely affects nonconsenting students in the DCSS, and, by virtue of the *stare decisis* doctrine, others like the "anti-busing" students in San Diego. *Amici*'s presentation is in the tradition of those in cases having serious imlications for nonparties. Compare *amicus* presentation in **Bob Jones University v. United States**, 461 U.S. 574 (1983).

Groundswell *Amici* then questioned the authority of the Circuit Court's order "to reassign DeKalb County students on a racial basis" to remedy "*de facto* 'segregation'," caused by residential patterns. It included the point that it was limited by the separation of powers provisions of the Constitution, concluding:

> ...Chief Justice Warren E. Burger reiterated in **Chadha** (**I.N.S. v. Chadha**, 462 U.S. 919 (1983)) *supra*, 462 U.S. at 951 that "(t)he Constitution sought to divide the delegated powers of the new federal government into three defined categories, Legislative, Executive and Judicial, to assure, as nearly as possible, that each Branch of government would confine itself to its assigned responsibility. He added that "(t)he hydraulic pressure inherent within each of the separate Branches to exceed the outer limits of its power, even to accomplish desirable objectives, must be resisted."
>
> This doctrine underlies, *Amici* submit, Chief Justice Burger's statement in **Swann** to the effect that there is no basis for ordering assignment of students on a racial basis to remedy *de facto* "segregation." Thus, the panel exceeds the outer limits of its power in ordering busing to remedy what, under the relevant facts and history, is at most *de facto* "segregation" in DeKalb County schools.

Groundswell's *amici* contention reasonably supports the above argument (p. 47) of Rex E. Lee, a former U.S. Solicitor General, on behalf of the petitioning DeKalb County School System when—

> ...Lee shifted gears and closed with a discussion of federalism and the efficient allocation of resources. Under **Dowell**, he said, school systems should be run by local governing bodies, and not federal courts. For 22 years, DCSS has been trying to obey the law, but now, due to circumstances beyond its control, its being told it will have to continue under court supervision for an indefinite length of time. Under the Eleventh Circuit's opinion, Lee noted, his clients are looking to more busing and radical gerrymandering....

Seven Civil Rights Groups file *Amici Curiae* Brief on Behalf of Respondents Pitts, Being the Class of Plaintiffs who Brought the Desegregation Class Action

An *Amici Curiae* brief was filed in support of the respondents Pitts, *et al*, a plaintiff-class of black students, by seven organizations, headed by the DeKalb County, Georgia, Branch of the NAACP, whose interest was stated as "representing individuals throughout the nation who share a critical interest in desegregation of public school systems."

The NAACP *Amici* Allegations in Support of Respondents' Class of Students were as follows:

> 1. DCSS' own inability to implement an effective plan of school desegregation during a period of increasing residential segregation cannot be invoked to remove judicial supervision over DCSS to ensure that it fulfills its constitutional duty to desegregate in the area of student assignment.
>
> 2. Effective desegregation must be accomplished simultaneously for a substantial period of years in all major areas of school system operations before a former *de jure* segregated school system such as DCSS should be released from judicial supervision.

Annexed to their brief as the Appendix is a document dated June 1991 entitled *School Desegregation: A Social Science Statement*. Among the many social scientists signing that statement were two who testified in the

Carlin case in support of mandatory student assignment as necessary and proper to achieve racial balance in San Diego schools.

At page 17a is a paragraph which epitomizes the objective of those *amici* organizations for judicially mandated student assignment, without using the term "busing," for as long as needed to "desegregate," as defined by them, a school system.

> The benefits of desegregation take place over the long term. When judicial requirements are unambiguous, and enforcement agencies promulgate precise regulations, desegregation is much more likely to succeed than when opposition leads judicial or agency principles to be stated in ambiguous or unclear terms. Schools that allow their desegregative goals to be derailed will often have paid the costs but not achieved the benefits of desegregation. Persistence allows schools to move past the period of community opposition and white flight, which may be strong within the first year of a plan but then decline rapidly.... (footnotes omitted).

Groundswell *Amici* Succeed in Placing the Personal Interest of Students Against Busing, in Contrast to the Impersonal Interest of a Class Favoring Busing, Before the Supreme Court

Groundswell *Amici* recognize in Civil Rights groups their sincere belief in, and effort to accomplish, the beneficence of desegregation. But its imposition is sought by autocratic judicial means, as in the **Freeman** case, exemplified by the above sociological statement filed in the case. Judicial requirements imposing "desegregation" until the community "opposition" acquiesces fall under the warning of Justice Louis D. Brandeis, dissenting in **Olmstead v. United States**, (1928) 277 U.S. 438 at 479:

> Experience should teach us to be most on our guard to protect liberty when the Government's purposes are beneficent. Men born to freedom are naturally alert to repel invasion of their liberty by evil-minded rulers. The greatest dangers to liberty lurk in the

> insidious encroachment by men of zeal, well meaning, but without understanding.

Two *amici curiae* presented the interest of black students against prejudicial racial gerrymandering of school boundaries by Pasadena school authorities in **Jackson v. Pasadena City School District**, *supra.* Although that issue was not before the California Supreme Court, it opined in that case a duty upon school boards to take reasonably feasible steps to alleviate racial imbalance in schools "regardless of cause."

The Groundswell interest of parents and students opposing busing is as appropriately presented as was the interest of black students in the **Jackson** case, and as well, to counter the reason posed by the social scientists for it. Groundswell **Amici** argued:

> In concluding that the DCSS "failed to fulfill its constitutional duties regarding student assignment," the panel makes an order which will require extensive mandatory busing. It concedes that to comply, "the DCSS's actions may be administratively awkward, inconvenient, and even bizarre in some situations and may impose burdens on some." **Pitts by Pitts**, *supra*, 887 F.2d at 1450…
>
> In the mandate's present form, the trial court is bound to fashion a plan so difficult to comply with as to "condemn a school district once governed by a board which intentionally discriminated to judicial tutelage for the indefinite future." **Board of Education of Oklahoma City Public Schools v. Dowell**, 111 S.Ct. 630,638 (1991). And during that period innocent, adversely affected students are to be subjected to loss of their constitutional rights, in violation of the Due Process Clause of the Fifth Amendment to the Constitution.

Annexed to the Groundswell brief is Appendix A, being copy of an exemplar, from Intervenors' Exhibit 6 for Identification in **Carlin v. Board of Education**, of petitions signed by 1,856 students objecting to mandatory racial school assignments. Their petitions, which in turn epitomize the position of the Groundswell *Amici*, each read:

> I, the undersigned child, residing in the San Diego Unified School District, respectfully object to school authorities making me, because of my race, go away from my neighborhood public school location to classes, without my consent and the consent of my parent(s), as a violation of my rights.

Thus, the Groundswell *Amici* voiced rights that they contend should be assertable by non-class persons when remedies adversely affecting them are judicially sought and imposed in a "desegregation" action for a particular class of persons.

CHALLENGE FOUR

SAN DIEGO INTERVENORS CHALLENGE COURT ASSSIGNMENT OF PUPILS IN CARLIN V. BOARD OF EDUCATION TOWARD RESTORING LOCAL CONTROL OF SAN DIEGO PUBLIC SCHOOLS

Upon the ruling in **Freeman** in addition to **Dowell**, Groundswell Intervenors now had a solid basis upon which to challenge continuing **Carlin** court jurisdiction, particularly over student assignment. But they ran into extremely strong opposition by their own school board, because the Defendant Board in the **Carlin** case now sided with the **Carlin** Plaintiffs in seeking to extend court jurisdiction indefinitely.

For this reason the Groundswell motions started right after **Freeman** took until December 15, 1995 to obtain an order terminating jurisdiction. Because Phase 5 of *Liberate Public Schools* details these motions and the opposition to them, they will be summarized here.

Second Motion to Terminate Jurisdiction

On April 6, 1992, Groundswell Intervenors moved to terminate court jurisdiction with a memorandum in support, relying strongly upon **Dowell** and **Freeman**, *supra*.

On May 20, 1992, in reversal of its 1981 position, the Board filed an opposition to the effect that the end of Court supervision could result in some loss of state integration funding support. Intervenors replied that the Board's speculative objection was not a legal basis for abdication of Board's jurisdiction.

The **Carlin** Class also opposed termination of the case arguing mainly that Board had not yet fully complied with the Writ of Mandate issued in 1977.

On May 28, 1992, the Court denied the motion.

Third Motion by Intervenors to Terminate Jurisdiction

Following denial of the second motion to terminate jurisdiction, another legal reason developed. Amendments to the Ralph W. Brown Act, Cal. Govt. Code, Secs. 54952.1, *et seq*., intended to "protect the right of the public to participate in local government" were enacted effective April 1, 1994.

On July, 22, 1994, the Intervenors for a third time moved to terminate court jurisdiction. They again cited the **Dowell** (1991) and **Freeman** (1992) decisions requiring termination of desegregation cases at the earliest practicable date; and that awaiting that time the non-class constituents of the Board were deprived of the governing participation to which they were lawfully entitled.

Intervenors emphasized that the Brown Act was designed to encourage constituents' participation. They gave the example that there had been no public input into the Board's immediate decision on April 7, 1992 in secret session under the Brown Act's litigation exception, to reverse its earlier decision and oppose the Intervenors' filing just a day earlier to terminate the case.

On September 21 and 27, 1994, the responses of the Board and Plaintiffs, respectively, were received in opposition to Intervenors' motion, reiterating that ending court supervision would cause a loss of state integration funding. Intervenors replied this was not a legal basis for continued jurisdiction.

To the contentions that the present "Final Order" should remain in effect, Groundswell Intervenors reiterated their earlier objection to the order's provision sanctioning student assignments solely because of their race and its implementation.

In conclusion, Intervenors cited in support of their motions, as well as the Los Angeles 1981 final order, **Spangler v. Pasadena City Bd. of Ed**., 611 F.2d 1239 (9th C.A., 1979) (trial court may not retain jurisdiction merely for matters of convenience); and **Dowell** (desegregation decrees are not intended to operate in perpetuity).

Intervenors also distinguished **Freeman** as pertaining to a school district under a desegregation order to establish a unitary system (whereas this district had always operated a unitary system); that when it had achieved a unitary status in the area of student assignments, court jurisdiction could be terminated in that area, although unitariness not yet established throughout the system.

On October 21, 1994 the Court denied the motion to terminate court jurisdiction, but did allow for the filing of a motion for reconsideration within ten days.

Motion for Reconsideration of Denial of Termination Request

A basis for a timely filed Motion for Reconsideration of the October 21 order was the need to respond to a filing by the Defendant Board of a supplemental memorandum "re: Grant of *Certiorari* by the United States Supreme Court in **Missouri v. Jenkins**." U.S. Supreme Ct. Docket No. 93-1823, 63 U.S.L.W. 3211 September 26, 1994.

Postponement, due to illness of Intervenors' counsel (the author), delayed argument until after the Supreme Court's reversal of the Circuit Court in **Missouri v. Jenkins**, supporting Intervenors' position in a broader way.

Senator Kopp Joins Motion as *Amicus Curiae*/Interested Person

For some time the author had been in touch with California State Senator Quentin L. Kopp requesting his support for the motion to terminate all court jurisdiction. On April 11, 1994, with the permission of the Court, the Senator filed his supporting brief as *Amicus Curiae* and, novelly, as an Interested Person, by invoking Section 7(a), Article I, of the California Constitution.

Amicus reiterated the points of Intervenors and emphasized prophetically from a legislator's point of view the unconstitutionality of race-balancing occurring in the Defendant's plan. He argued that non-class constituents in the District were denied the democratic rights available to their counterparts in Los Angeles and other districts not under court supervision. He further noted this was a district absent a constitutional violation on its part, without which federal decisions had held there is no basis for assigning students on a racial basis, citing **Swann v. Charlotte-Mecklenburg Board of Education** (1971), 402 U.S. 1 at 28.

Amicus argued that in this district there was no basis for extended court supervision to achieve racial balancing, quoting Justice Scalia, in concurrence in **Freeman** (1992), 112 S.Ct. 1430, at 1450-51:

> "The District Court in the present case found that the imbalances in student assignment were attributable to private demographic shifts rather than governmental action. Without disturbing this finding, and without finding that revision of student assignments was necessary to remedy some other unlawful government action, the Court of Appeals ordered DeKalb County to institute massive busing and other programs to achieve integration. The Court convincingly demonstrates that this cannot be reconciled with our cases, and I join its opinion....
>
> Almost a quarter-century ago, in **Green v. School Bd.**, New Kent County, 391 U.S. 430, 437-438...(1968), this Court held that school systems which had been enforcing *de jure* segregation at the time of **Brown I** had not merely an obligation to assign students and resources on a race-neutral basis but also an 'affirmative duty' to 'desegregate,' that is to achieve insofar as practicable racial balance in their schools. This holding has become such a part of our legal fabric that there is a tendency, reflected in the Court of Appeals opinion in this case, to speak as though the Constitution requires such racial balancing. Of course it does not: The Equal Protection Clause reaches only those racial imbalances shown to be intentionally caused by the State...."

New Facts and Law Support Reconsideration

For the hearing on the Motion for Reconsideration, rescheduled December 15, 1995, intervening events were summarized for the Court in a supplemental memorandum, the key event being the rendering on June 12, 1995 of **Missouri v. Jenkins,** 115 S.Ct. 2033, 132 L.Ed 2d 63.

Intervenors also argued that **Jenkins** made it clear that **Freeman** offered no support for the retention of judicial jurisdiction until the academic goals sought in behalf of minority students were met in that case, quoting Chief Justice Rehnquist:

> "Insistence upon academic goals unrelated to the effects of legal segregation unwarrantably postpones the day when the

KCMSD will be able to operate on its own." 115 S.Ct. 2056, 132 L Ed 2d 89.

Finally, Intervenors asserted that the Supreme Court decided the issues in **Jenkins** in favor of Groundswell in reversing the Eighth Circuit:

> "On remand, the District Court must bear in mind that its end purpose is not only 'to remedy the violation' to the extent practicable, *but also 'to restore state and local authorities to the control of a school system that is operating in compliance with the Constitution.*' **Freeman** *supra*, at 489." (Emphasis added)

Upon Reconsideration Court Grants Motion to Terminate Jurisdiction

On December 15, 1995, the Court granted the Groundswell motion to terminate court jurisdiction and discharge the writ of mandate, and gave the parties six months to prepare for finalizing a final order at that time. The ruling was construed by Intervenors as one which would then approve a modified integration order, after input by counsel, and finally terminate jurisdiction by discharging the writ of mandate along the lines of the **Crawford** order.

However, by the time of the hearing on July 26, 1996 of the Final Order Terminating Court Jurisdiction, the Defendant School Board and **Carlin** Plaintiffs took the opposing position that the final order should continue court supervisory orders without discharging the writ of mandate.

Phase 5 of *Liberate Public Schools* details the exchange of views regarding the contents between the Groundswell Intervenors and those of the Defendant School Board and **Carlin** Plaintiffs, summarized as follows.

Groundswell Intervenors Seek Final Order in Compliance with Current Constitutional Rulings and Discharging Writ of Mandate

In their first memorandum on March 14, 1996, Groundswell Intervenors urged that the order to be presented re: the integration plan require that the plan meet current constitutional standards.

The first point was that **Missouri v. Jenkins**, coming after the motion for reconsideration, was a guide in terminating these proceedings. For that case made it clear that **Freeman** offered no support for contentions that judicial jurisdiction could be retained until the academic goals sought in behalf of "minority" students were met in the absence of a finding of a constitutional violation by this school district. Accordingly, it was incumbent upon the Board to see that the school system being restored to its control operated in compliance with the Constitution.

The second point was that the San Diego school system must discontinue racial balancing to be in compliance with the Constitution. This was also incompatible with the best educational interests of "minorities" by reason of a conflict of interest with their attorneys. Intervenors argued the conflict arose in the following manner:

> The record shows that Plaintiffs are represented by civil rights attorneys (ACLU) within the meaning of the article "Serving Two Masters: Integration Ideals and Client Interest in School Desegregation Litigation," by Derrick A. Bell, Jr., in *The Yale Law Journal*, vol. 85: 470, 1976. Professor Bell points out the conflict of interest between the integration ideals of civil rights attorneys via race balancing, and the espousal of educational improvement by the minorities they purport to represent....

On May 14, 1996, Groundswell in a second brief referred to their March 18, 1996, brief calling for the presentation of a plan which would not carry forward the unconstitutional features in, and underlying, the present plan, mandating race balancing.

Accordingly, Intervenors urged the Board to return to its 1981 position when it proposed final approval of a voluntary integration plan, based upon the precedential ruling by Judge Lopez terminating the **Crawford** case on September 10, 1981.

Groundswell Presents Objections re: the Integration Plan to the Board on May 23 and 30, 1996

In the meantime the Board had set public hearings on its integration plan, to which Groundswell Intervenors came to believe were designed to support Board's position favoring indefinite continuance of court supervision.

Intervenors prepared presentations which summarized the objections to the plan spelled out in the foregoing two briefs to be made in behalf of Groundswell by its president to the Board at its scheduled meetings.

On May 23 and May 30, 1996, Mr. Lester presented those objections to the Board, a written summary of which was given to each Board member. He called to their attention 63 signatories on petitions presented earlier objecting to the assignment of students *solely* on the basis of race, as being unconstitutional and not taking into account the individual educational needs of the students so assigned.

Reasons for believing Groundswell's objections were not fairly treated are spelled out in Phase 5 of *Liberate Public Schools*. Primarily, there was an untimely declaration advising the court of majority public support for the integration plan that did not fairly depict the position of Intervenors by omitting reference to objecting petitions on file with the Board. Those objections were to the involuntary discriminatory aspects of the present program, not to an integration plan conforming to the Constitution.

Groundswell Intervenors Propose Final Order With Finality; While Other Parties' Proposals Lack Finality, as Does the "Final" Order Adopted by the Court

On July 11, 1996, Groundswell Intervenors proposed the Court find the racial balancing presently existing; conclude its implementation should be discontinued as unconstitutional; and provide for Discharge of the Writ of Mandate.

Just before July 14, forms of final order were proposed by the Plaintiffs and Board. Each proposed "final" order extended indefinitely the jurisdiction of the Court by failing to provide for discharge of the writ of mandate.

Board's memorandum argued that magnet eligibility and classroom balance rules did not impermissibly discriminate on the basis of race, citing principally **Crawford I** and **Bakke**.

The Plaintiffs' proposal similarly made no reference to a termination date. It dismissed Groundswell's objection to student assignment to particular seats and classrooms solely on the basis of race as without merit. It argued "this Court's jurisdiction arises under the California Constitution and not under federal law," citing **Crawford I** in support.

On July 26, 1996, the **Carlin** Plaintiffs, the Defendant Board, the Groundswell Intervenors and the proposed Nixon Intervenors, with their respective counsel and supporters, appeared before the Court. All had filed memoranda and numerous declarations in support of their positions; and State Senator Kopp and State Assemblyman Steve Baldwin had filed briefs as *Amici Curiae* and Interested Persons in support of Groundswell.

The Court approved the proposals of the **Carlin** Plaintiffs and the Board (district) as follows:

> THE COURT: ...So I—I think the order that—the exit order that I will approve would be the plaintiffs' proposed orders, which, except for Paragraphs 1, 2 and 25 mirror the District's; and would provide in Paragraph 25 of that order as the last sentence to say that "these orders shall terminate and be of no force and effect after January 1, 2000."

On August 16, 1996, the "Final" Order Terminating Court Jurisdiction was filed. The first 20 paragraphs ordered the District to take certain educational steps, focusing upon "racial/ethnic" groups, and continued approval of racial assignments.

The Groundswell Intervenors unsuccessfully sought appellate writ of mandate to speed the end of the **Carlin** case, but a petition to the Fourth District Court of Appeal was denied on November 18, 1996; the California Supreme Court denied review on January 17, 1997.

At that time any unfunded effort to terminate court jurisdiction before January 1, 2000 appeared futile in the face of powerful dual opposition. But Groundswell's attorney saw an earlier possibility if the California Civil Rights Initiative (Proposition 209) was upheld, as constitutional, on a pending appeal to the Ninth Circuit Court of Appeals from a U.S. District Court ruling. All counsel in the **Carlin** case had been watching Proposition 209, which was on the ballot November 5, 1996 at the time of the hearing July 26, 1996 on the adoption of a Final Order.

The Board saw the possibility of Prop. 209 going into effect as a reason for indefinite court juridiction, by making this extraordinary admission in Footnote 7 of its July 19, 1996 brief:

> ...Pursuant to the language of that proposed initiative (Prop. 209), it could be illegal for the District to continue to take race and ethnic status into account in its integration program. There is, however, an exception for such actions pursuant to "pre-existing" Court Orders. Under the circumstances, the existence of this proposed initiative is yet another reason why the District seeks this Final Order as proposed.

This signified a determination to continue racial assignments of non-class students under its integration program, immunized from charges by Intervenors of illegality under Proposition 209.

Intervenors contrarily saw that racial assignments until January 1, 2000 and beyond would place non-class students in a position of being unable to assert constitutional rights, in a manner disapproved in **Goss v. Lopez**, (1975) 419 U.S. 565,574:

> Although Ohio may not be constitutionally obligated to establish and maintain a public school system, it has nevertheless done so and has required its children to attend. Those young people do not "shed their constitutional rights at the schoolhouse door."

San Diego students should not have to shed the right, which their counterparts have in other California districts not under a court order, to challenge their assignments as unconstitutional.

CHALLENGE FIVE

SAN DIEGANS CHALLENGE PERPETUAL COURT ASSIGNMENT OF PUPILS, EMANATING FROM <u>CARLIN V. BOARD OF EDUCATION</u>, TO RESTORE LOCAL CONTROL ACCORDING TO THE CONSTITUTION

United States Court of Appeals Upholds Proposition 209

On April 8, 1997, a Ninth Circuit Panel upheld the California Civil Rights Initiative (Proposition 209), adopted by Californians as Article I, Section 31, to their Constitution,
providing in relevant part:

> "The State shall not discriminate against, or grant preferential treatment to, any individual or group on the basis of race, sex, color, ethnicity, or national origin in the operation of... public education…." **Coalition for Econ. Equity v. Wilson**, 110 F.3d 1431, 1434 (9th Cir.1997).

Accordingly, Groundswell Intervenors prepared a fourth motion for an order to terminate jurisdiction, along with an order that the Board modify its integration program to comply with current constitutional standards. After a telephonic conference on July 14, 1997, Groundswell secured a meaningful open court hearing of the motion. **Armstrong v. Manzo** (1965), 380 U.S. 545,550,552.

Fourth Motion Succeeds in Conditional Advancement of Judicial Termination Date to July 1, 1998

On August 22, 1997 Groundswell motions were heard, supported by a separate brief by *Amicus* Senator Kopp, who was a sponsor of Proposition 209. There were two basic points, after emphasizing the recent upholding of Proposition 209 by the Ninth Circuit Panel.

First, that the Court should order the Board to modify its integration plan to bring it into constitutional compliance with current law and facts by ending (a) mandatory racial ratios and (b) racial boundary gerrymandering to racially balance classrooms and schools.

Second, that the Court should restore to the people jurisdiction over a constitutionally-operated system as required by federal decisional law, reciting **Dowell** and **Freeman**.

The Board reiterated its earlier opposition, as did Plaintiffs. Both stressed that the constitutionality of Proposition 209 was still at issue, and that even if it was upheld there was a specific exception for preexisting court orders.

The Judge, after argument, denied Intervenors' request to order modifications in the existing final order, but conditionally advanced the termination of jurisdiction date from January 1, 2000 to July 1, 1998 provided Proposition 209 was upheld by then by the Supreme Court. On September 5, 1997, the Order Modifying Final Order Terminating Court Jurisdiction was filed, making just that one change in the Final Order. Proposition 209 was upheld by the Supreme Court on November 3, 1997.

Board Unsuccessfully Petitions the California Fourth District Court of Appeal to Reinstate Termination Date of January 1, 2000

On October 21, 1997 the Board filed a Petition to the Court of Appeal for Writ of Mandate or Prohibition, with a massive set of exhibits. It sought "review of the portion of Respondent San Diego Superior Court's September 5, 1997 Order which modified its prior August 1996 Final Order and set an earlier date for terminating Court jurisdiction in this school integration case."

On November 19, 1997 the Court of Appeal ordered the Superior Court (by real party in interest Groundswell) to show cause by December

1 why the relief requested should not be granted; petitioner Board to reply by December 8, 1997.

On December 1, the Response of Groundswell argued that extraordinary relief was not warranted because abdication of jurisdiction by the Board (1) lacked a legal basis and (2) inequitably denied Intervenors of their civil rights under Proposition 209 and other laws. It concluded that the Order Modifying the Final Order was in line with federal decisional law:

> ...The most recent federal desegregation decisions emphasize the importance of "(r)eturning schools to the control of local authorities at the earliest practicable date (as) essential to restore their true accountability in our governmental system." **Freeman** (1992), *supra*, 118 L.Ed. 108 2d. at 134. *See also* **Board of Educ. of Oklahoma City P. Sch. v. Dowell**, 111 S.Ct. 630,638 (1991)....

On December 8, the Los Angeles Unified School District and the California Voluntary Integration Association each received permission and filed *amicus curiae* briefs supporting the Board.

Fourth District Court of Appeal Sustains Trial Court's Order Terminating Jurisdiction

On January 10, 1998, counsel for the Board and the **Carlin** Plaintiffs argued in support of the Board's Petition to Mandate reinstatement of the January 1, 2001 date of termination; while Enstrom, for Groundswell Intervenors, opposed the petition.

On February 9, 1998 the District Court of Appeal rendered its decision in **Board of Education v. Superior Court**, 61 Cal. App.4th 411 (Feb. 1998), denying the Petition for Writ of Mandate. The Court at 61 Cal.App.4th 419 cited favorably the cases of great signifance to Groundswell, namely **Dowell** (498 U.S. 237,238) and **Freeman** (503 U.S. 467,489), emphasizing prompt return of local control to a school system that is operating in compliance with the Constitution.

The Court also noted the importance of the termination of jurisdiction to Groundswell parents and their children:

> Groundswell objected to any further extension of jurisdiction, claiming "(f)or each day that the present 'Final Order' remains in effect, non-class constituents... will be unable to exercise their civil rights under (Section 31 (Proposition 209)) and independently applicable civil rights laws in a manner similar to their counterparts elsewhere not under the constraints of a court order." 61 Cal.App.4th at 417.

The Appellate Court concluded:

> In sum, although the (Superior) court acknowledged Section 31's (Proposition 209) adoption in ruling on Groundswell's motion, the court did not conclude the section compelled it to modify its previous order. Rather, the court reviewed the action in the context of new law to revisit its prior order. Having considered it, along with other factors, the court concluded the historical basis for the court's involvement no longer existed; District had demonstrated its commitment to desegregation; continued court supervision was no longer necessary to compel compliance with constitutional obligations; and control should be returned to District. Based on these findings, the court did not abuse its discretion in accelerating the end of supervision. *Id.* at 422.

This was a return to local control by gaining the right of "non-class" San Diego citizens to participate on an equal basis with those formerly in the preferred "class" as defined in the **Carlin** class action. But it left undisturbed the denial by Superior Court of the portion of Groundswell's motion to eliminate consideration of race in certain programs to bring the integration program into compliance with current federal decisional law.

That the Board and Plaintiffs sought to retain in the integration program the objected-to racial aspects was evidenced by their opposition to the discharge of the 1977 writ of mandate in the **Carlin** case. So Groundswell's next step necessarily was to obtain an order discharging the Writ of Mandate. This would make it possible to assert the unconstitutionality of those aspects of the challenged programs free of any inhibition alleged by reason of a pending court order.

Groundswell Motion to Discharge Writ of Mandate is Granted, Effective July 1, 1998

On July 28, 1998 Groundswell filed a Motion That Court Issue an Order Discharging as of July 1, 1998 the Writ of Mandate. It recited that the Petition in *Mandamus* by the Board to the Fourth District Court of Appeal to return the termination date January 1, 2000 had been denied on February 9, 1998, but the writ of mandate remained to be discharged.

On August 26, 1998 the Court granted the Motion to Discharge the Writ of Mandate in a manner which did not change the judicial directions as to the Board's integration plan in the Final Order, as is seen from the formal order (filed September 30, 1998):

> IT IS ORDERED that the Writ of Mandate issued as of March 10, 1977 is discharged as of July 1, 1998. The Court's August 1996 Order directed the District to continue and to increase its integration programs and goals. Significantly, no party appealed that Order and it remains viable. If future actions warrant involvement, the Court's jurisdiction can be invoked again by a new Writ of Mandate.

The Groundswell parents and their children, with the author as their *pro bono* counsel, had achieved local control in the sense they and other San Diegans similarly situated were now free of a non-class status in a pending class action. They could now exercise the full range of their civil rights on a level "playing field." It remained to be seen how the Board would respond to the following modifications in the integration plan they had sought, but which were not granted, in the Final Order:

> (E)liminate the use of racial and ethnic considerations in connection with its "classroom balance," "Voluntary Ethnic Enrollment Program (VEEP)," "Choice" programs, and the establishment of school attendance zones.

The Board Proposes Modifications in Its Integration Plan, But Retains Underlying Racial Considerations While Disclaiming Them

On October 20, 1999, the San Diego Board advised of proposed modifications to its Integration Plan in an article by its counsel titled "A Different Approach" in the *Union-Tribune*:

> ...The district is now proposing changes that would remove a student's race/ethnicity as a criterion for eligibility to attend schools outside of the student's area of residence. The changes would encompass a system of choice and selection that avoids race-based consideration while using factors such as geography and residential patterns to continue nurturing integrated schools. The proposal would by no means lessen the district's commitment to diversity....

The Board's proposals did not meet Groundswell objections that they were not race-neutral in line with recent federal decisions. Nor did a final proposal meet the objections which the author placed before the Board on November 30, 1999.

Enstrom presented examples of objections by non-class constituents of the Board in the **Carlin** case opposing the future use of race/ethnicity in its integration proposal. One objection, and the basis for it, was by a minority-classified student originally excluded from a magnet school because of her race and residence, by way of a copy of her written statement to the Board:

> My name is Kimberly... I live in University City. I attend Marcy Elementary and I am in the 6th grade. Math and Reading are my best subjects but I love drama the best. I have been in a few plays at my school but I wish to be in more plays. I found out there is a special school called the School of Creative and Performing Arts. My mom sent in an application to ask if I could go but they said "No." Then my mom sent another application to Gompers and they also said "No, I can not go." They said I couldn't go because I am not the right color, I don't live in the right neighborhood, and I would hurt the racial balance. I think that this is not fair because God made children the same, so we should be treated the same. We

> should *Not* be treated according to our skin color, or where we live, or what Ethnic group we are. Why do you treat children according to their skin color, or where they live, or what Ethnic group they are. I don't understand why you are treating children like this?

Enstrom recommended a race-neutral plan in which the Board's objective should be to provide the best quality of education to all the students with its top priority being the quality of the local schools. The plan adopted should eliminate both race/ethnicity *and* residence of applicants in their selection, by a random drawing process, to any school (legitimately boundaried and appropriately available) for which there were more applicants than spaces available.

When it appeared racial gerrymandering would continue, albeit subtlely, in the plan to be adopted, the author made one final objection in a "Viewpoint" entitled "Stop Racial Balancing," published January 10, 2000 in the San Diego *Daily Transcript*. Appendix 3 to *Liberate Public Schools*. In it, he illustrated the manner in which the plan retained racial considerations in both the Magnet Program and Voluntary Ethnic Enrollment Program (VEEP) while stating it was eliminating them.

In Paragraph 5, he referred to the Magnet Program:

> As to magnet eligibility, the proposed cluster formula is designed to advance race-balancing by the racial gerrymandering of the District into four clusters based upon the number of white students in them, with the highest number being in Cluster 1, declining in Clusters 2 and 3 to the lowest number in Cluster 4. Conversely, the lowest number of students classified as "minorities" is in Cluster 1, increasing in Clusters 2 and 3 to the highest number in Cluster 4. Priorities in applications to attend a Magnet school are assigned according the respective locations of the applicant and the school.

In Paragraph 6, he then illustrated that if a child of the same age, race and location as Kimberly were to apply under the proposed plan to the same magnet school, she would still have less priority to attend than a child living in a different cluster gerrymandered to promote racial balancing.

As to VEEP eligibility, Paragraphs 6 and 7, *Id.*, Appendix 3, it was illustrated that under the proposed plan a child able to walk to a neighborhood school could again have less priority to attend that school than a VEEP child, bused free from many miles away, by reason of racially gerrymandered school boundaries to accomplish racial balancing.

On January 25 the Board adopted a new Integration Plan headlined "S.D. magnet schools will drop race as a criterion." *Id.*, Appendix 4. Regardless of the objections, apparently this plan will use boundaries as racially clustered for magnet school assignments and as drawn by the District for VEEP school assignments. Thereby, applicants to schools participating in the magnet and VEEP programs will be given priority according to their residences, as may be gleaned from a close reading of the news report of the plan in Appendix 4 to *Liberate Public Schools*, and the following statement by the District's integration program manager reflecting the relation of race to the residence of applicants (*Id*, para.6);

> The challenge has been in creating a program that eliminates race as a criteria but would not segregate our schools... I think *you will find a close correlation across the country between race, socioeconomics and geography.* (Emphasis added)

Thus, unless corrected, San Diego students may await their assignments in coming years under a program whose manager states it is eliminating "race as a criteria (*sic*)", but in which it comes into play by reason of its correlation with "socioeconomics and geography." The implementation of such a program should be subjected to close scrutiny under applicable facts and law.

Study of the Facts

Salient facts faced the Board at the end of the **Carlin** case. The population of the classified "White," majority-treated, students had dropped from 76% at the start of the case in 1967 to about 30% at its end on July 1, 1998; and that of the classified "Non-White," minority-treated, students had increased conversely. District records showed that "African-Americans" and "Hispanics" grouped in the "Non-White" category were not testing academically as high as students classified as "Whites," following racial balancing at the demand of the **Carlin** Plaintiff Class for the preceding twenty years.

Additionally, the Board was confronted with rooting out of existence on July 1, 1998, administrative procedures for assigning students on the basis of race to racially balance schools, classrooms and seats within classroons. Groundswell cited **Adarand Constructors, Inc. v Pena**, 115 S.Ct. 2097 (1995) as requiring elimination of the following procedures.

1. A *Basic Rule* mandating racially balanced classrooms.
2. VEEP *Administrative Procedures* defining racially imbalanced schools, monitoring enrollments, and "work(ing) with that school in implementing an action plan to assure a 50/50 balance…."
3. *District Procedures re: Establishment and Change of Attendance Areas Criteria* setting boundaries with precedence to "a. Racial and Ethnic Balance" and failing in the remaining "b" to "h" criteria to include the most important criterion of "proximity" of the family home to the school.

Study of the Law

We next look at some briefly described modes of racial discrimination nullified recently as unconstitutional, to alert a careful study of the facts, conclusions and decisions in the various cases according to the readers' interests.

> 7-year old white Jacob Eisenberg successfully challenged denial of his request to go to a magnet school because of "its impact on diversity." Underlying the notice was the determination of the school board to achieve racial balance in its schools in accordance with its countywide population. In effect, his request was denied on the basis of his race. **Montgomery County Public Schools v. Eisenberg**, 197 F.3d 123 (4th Cir. 1999). Reversed **Eisenberg v. Montgomery County Public Schools**, 19 F.Supp.2d 449 (D.Md. 1998). *Certiorari* denied 2000 U.S.Lexis 1925 (3/20/00). Compare **Tuttle v. Arlington County School Board**, 195 F.3d 698 (4th Cir. 1999).
>
> Teen white Sarah Wessmann sucessfully challenged denial of

> admission to Boston Latin School, which allocated the second half of available seats on the basis of "flexible racial/ethnic guidelines" which apportioned them to five different racial/ethnic categories. But the number admitted in rank order from each of the five categories for these remaining spots had to match the proportion set by school officials for that category. Because the proportion set for "Whites" was filled, Sarah and other score-qualified applicants were passed over to admit lower-score ranked applicants, classified as Blacks and Hispanics, for admission. **Wessmann v. Gittens**, 160 F.3d 790 (1st Cir.1998). Reversed **Wessmann by Wessmann v. Boston School Committee**, 996 F.Supp. 120 (D.Mass. 1998).
>
> Four white students successfully challenged the admissions process the University of Texas School of Law employed in 1992, which granted racial preferences to Blacks and Mexican Americans by means of a separate admissions track. **Hopwood v. State of Texas**, 84 F.3d 720 (5th Cir., 1996). Reversed **Hopwood v. State of Texas**, 861 F.Supp. 551 (W.D.Tex.1994).

Groundswell citizens have continuously emphasized the principle enunciated by Chief Justice Warren in his *Memoirs* (pp.287-8), that "any kind of racial discrimination in public education is unconstituional." By analogy, black citizens once faced racial discrimination by a state statute requiring registration for voting, without mentioning race, in such a way that effectively resulted in a failure of such citizens to register and thereby be prevented from ever entering the voting booths.

This earlier kind of racial discrimination, effectively depriving a class of citizens of their voting rights, was found unconstitutional in **Lane v. Wilson**, 307 U.S. 268 (1939). Justice Felix Frankfurter, applying the 15th Amendment (307 U.S. at 276), portended the constitutional scrutiny (under the 14th Amendment), facing present-day racial discrimination in public schools:

> "The Amendment nullifies sophisticated as well as simple-minded modes of discrimination."

CHALLENGE SIX

PARENTS CAN CHALLENGE PERPETUAL COURT ASSIGNMENT OF PUPILS, IN PENDING CLASS ACTIONS, TOWARD RESTORING LOCAL CONTROL ACCORDING TO THE CONSTITUTION

The "Groundswell" parents challenged the **Carlin** Court assignment of San Diego children from the time it was assumed on March 10, 1977 until, with their counsel, they ended that case and restored local control July 1, 1998. The success of the Groundswell Intervenors, hopefully, can encourage equally dedicated parents toward restoring local control of assignment of their children now under court control in over four hundred class actions.

The key to Groundswell success was the conjoining of the parents and their counsel in their reliance upon the Constitution in restoring local control of the public education of San Diego students.

Groundswell Parents and Their Counsel Rely Upon the Constitution in Regaining in Local Control of Public School Student Assignment in San Diego

The San Diego parent effort in behalf of local control began after the court mandate March 10, 1977 that their school board take additional steps to "alleviate (*de facto*) segregation." In late spring, 1977, their school board held a series of meetings, the tenor of which was described by the Groundswell leader as "get ready because it's (busing) coming and there is nothing you can do about it." Their response that summer was to gather, and then present to their U.S. Representative, over 22,300 signatories for a Neighborhood Schools Amendment to the Constitution including a provision that "(no) student shall be compelled to attend public school other than the one nearest his residence…." Although these early petitioners did not produce results, they continued to exercise First

Amendment rights by petitions opposing racial assignments presented to the school board and then to the Court by their counsel.

About the same time petitions for a Neighborhood Schools Amendment were gathered for congressional action, a commentary was published by Author Enstrom on September 18, 1977 in *The San Diego Union* entitled "Busing, Not Integration, Opposed." He had been reading the **Carlin** trial reports in that paper, while questioning the extraordinary judicial power being sought to racially balance San Diego schools. For instance, **Carlin** counsel on January 25, 1977 demanded the involuntary racial assignments of non-class, innocent children, who lacked direct representation in this class action:

> The "time for voluntary plans is over... they only postpone the inevitable...." (counsel for Carlin Plaintiffs).
>
> (The court) asked, "Do you think that it is the duty of the district (to desegregate the schools) no matter what the price to individual children... the law must march on?"
>
> "A difficult question, but yes, the law marches on...." (counsel for Carlin Plaintiffs).

Concerns that such involuntary integration plans were unlawful and counter-productive, as contrasted to lawful, voluntary integration, were expressed in Enstrom's commentary titled "Busing, Not Integration, Opposed." During the period following its publication the Groundswell group strongly supported that position and importuned him to represent them. Upon their inability to retain counsel, Enstrom undertook *pro bono* representation on May 12, 1979, as detailed in *Busing—Not Integration—Opposed* (pp.22,25) and *Liberate Public Schools* (pp.24-25).

This *Handbook* sums up the challenges, chronicled in its Introduction, met by Groundswell parents and their counsel in his representation to return local control of San Diego schools. This representation took off with their *amici curiae* brief, filed October 10, 1980, setting forth their constitutional objections to **Carlin** Plaintiffs' motion for the mandatory assignment of the Groundswell children on a racial basis for racial balancing purposes. This brief emphasized that the children to be so assigned and their parents were the real parties in interest, and were constitutionally entitled to separate representation. It is annexed as the

Appendix to this *Handbook*.

The benefit of the return of local control in San Diego has been immediately seen by the Board's proposal to its constituents for modifications as to the assignment of students. No longer could voiced concerns by parents to the school assignments of their children be unheeded by a school board as bound by a pending court ruling.

As in Oklahoma City and DeKalb County, Georgia, San Diego parents can now meaningfully express their views to an elected board of education as to student assignment in the republican form of government—local control—designed for their education. The Supreme Court decisions in **Dowell** and **Freeman** offer a constitutional basis for similarly restoring local control to the thousands of parents in the hundreds of class actions remaining under court supervision.

Other Parents, with their Counsel, can rely upon the Constitution to Restore Local Control of Student Assignment From Class Actions

Groundswell parents and their children—not the school board being sued—were the real parties in interest concerning judicial assignment of their children. They lacked the finances to necessarily oppose it in court but their right to constitutionally oppose it was eagerly asserted by their *pro bono* lawyer-parent. This dedication to restoration of local control of the education of their children according to the Constitution is shared with such parents by many parent-lawyers. For this and other reasons set forth in the Conclusion, such parents can anticipate a similar response of *pro bono* assistance, if needed, aided by the experience of the Groundswell parents.

It will depend upon such parents to obtain such lawyers, in many cases, to regain local control of the education of their children from class actions against their school boards, to which they are not parties. For they must first gain legal representation to present their special interest in local control where, over ten years after **Dowell**, it appears few school boards have tried to terminate court supervision.

The efforts of parents and their legal counsel to restore the democratic processes in their public school districts will not be easy, as is pointed out by Supreme Court Justice Antonin Scalia in his concurring opinion in

Freeman v. Pitts, 112 S.Ct. 1430 at 1450:

> Our decision will be of great assistance to the citizens of DeKalb County, who for the first time since 1969 will be able to run their own public schools, at least so far as student assignments are concerned. It will have little effect, however, upon the many other school districts throughout the country that are still being supervised by federal judges, since it turns upon the extraordinarily rare circumstance of a *finding* that no portion of the current racial imbalance is a remnant of prior *de jure* discrimination. While it is perfectly appropriate for the Court to decide this case on that narrow basis, we must resolve—if not today, then soon—what is to be done in the vast majority of other districts, where, though our cases continue to profess that judicial oversight of school operations is a temporary expedient, democratic processes remain suspended, with no prospect of restoration, 38 years after **Brown v. Board of Education**...
>
> ...Since a multitude of private factors has shaped school systems in the years after abandoment of *de jure* segregation... the percentage of the current makeup of school systems attributable to the prior, government-enforced discrimination has diminished with each passing year, to the point where it cannot realistically be assumed to be a significant factor. 112 S.Ct. at 1453.
>
> At some time, we must acknowledge that it has become absurd to assume, without any further proof, that violations of the Constitution, dating from the days when Lyndon Johnson was President, or earlier, continue to have an appreciable effect upon current operation of schools. We are close to that time. While we must continue to prohibit, without qualification, all racial discrimination in the operation of public schools, and to afford remedies that eliminate not only the discrimination but its identified consequences, we should consider laying aside the extraordinary, and increasingly counterfactual, presumption of **Green**. We must soon revert to the ordinary principles of our law, of our democratic heritage, and our educational tradition: that plaintiffs alleging Equal Protection violations must prove intent and causation and not merely the existence of racial disparity

> (citations omitted); that public schooling, even in the South, should be controlled by locally elected authorities acting in conjunction with parents (citations omitted); and that it is "desirable" to permit pupils to attend schools nearest their homes…." 112 S.Ct. 1453,54.

This concurring opinion points out the difficulties in ending court supervision facing school boards whose predecessors had *de jure* segregated schools before desegregation actions were filed against them in the mid 1960s or earlier. As stated, before being released from court supervision in these actions, these school boards have to overcome the "increasingly counter factual presumption of **Green**."

The **Green** presumption requires current boards to obtain "a *finding* that no portion of the current racial imbalance is a remnant of prior *de jure* discrimination." As pointed out, it unduly encumbers, under current circumstances, boards in endeavoring to end court supervision.

One can see the reason for this opinion's concern in the burden placed upon the school board in DeKalb County School System by the Eleventh Circuit ruling on appeal in **Freeman**. For it ruled DCSS would not achieve unitary status "until it maintains at least three years of racial equality in (the six **Green**) categories: student assignment, faculty, staff, transportation, extracurricular activities, and facilities." After 20 years of court supervision, the Eleventh Circuit concluded, "DCSS continues to operate racially identifiable schools. The DCSS has never achieved unitary status and it retains the duty to eliminate all vestiges of the dual school system." *See* Argument before Supreme Court in **Freeman v. Pitts**, Challenge Three, *supra*, pp.47-49.

Fortunately for parents dedicated to local control, the high court overruled the Eleventh Circuit and upheld the trial court's ruling that DCSS had met its duty to the extent practicable as to the **Green** category of sudent assignment, and released it from court supervision. It further held the district court has the authority to relinquish supervision and control over a school district in incremental stages before full compliance has been achieved in every (**Green**) area of school operations.

Especially encouraging to parents seeking return of local control over student assignment at the earliest practicable date were these words in Justice Anthony M. Kennedy's majority opinion:

> Returning schools to the control of local authorities at the earliest practicable date is essential to restore their true accountability in our governmental system. **Freeman v. Pitts**, 503 U.S. 467,489.

This signals that parents, who believe their school districts have gained unitary status in student assignment, can take action toward ending court supervision in that category. Their most effective action may be by their first gaining counsel and, following the example of the Groundswell parents, then gaining a voice before the trial court as *amici curiae*. *See* Appendix. Such a brief could establish that they are the real parties in interest in this category. It could request the trial court, with its inherent power to control its calender, to order the parties to show cause why court control over student assignment should not be ended in the interest of justice.

Parent interest in their children's public school assignment is such that they are the real parties in interest in the category of student assignment and thus are entitled to assert it. Groundswell parents initially asserted it as friends of the **Carlin** Court in an *amici curiae* brief, annexed as the Appendix, and reasserted it as intervenors at the trial. Challenge Two, *supra*, pp.34-40. Their intervention first as *amici curiae* and then as intervenors laid the foundation for their ultimately restoring local control to San Diego schools.

Class Action Immunization of Racially Discriminatory Student Assignments Should Not Continue Indefinitely

The Los Angeles school board on September 12, 1980 in **Board of Ed., Etc. v. Superior Court** unsuccessfully sought a Supreme Court Justice to stay the massive reassignments of Los Angeles students court-ordered for September 16, 1980. The status of the case was such that its argument was limited to the "white flight" burden upon the district, rather than the unlawful burden upon the indididual students and their parents:

> ...The board's primary contention here is that "white flight," which all parties concede has taken place in the school district, will accelerate if this plan is put into effect... 448 U.S. at 1347.

Such unsuccessful arguments show the need for adversely affected students, of all races, to have a direct voice in these cases, for attempts by school boards to otherwise present their views have been ruled irrelevant. *See* **Monroe v. Board of Com'rs of City of Jackson, Tenn**. 391 U.S. 450,459 (1968). At the July 16, 1981 **Carlin** trial, objections by the intervening Groundswell parents and students to busing were similarly ruled irrelevant (Challenge Two, *supra*, pp.35-40), but there was no appeal to challenge that ruling.

In **Crawford III**, Bustop, Inc., an intervening nonprofit corporation, presented separate objections to the Supreme Court, in behalf of a Los Angeles group to the racial reassignments of students in that district, which the Court did not reach:

> Respondent Bustop, Inc., argues that far from doing "more" than the Fourteenth Amendment requires. the State actually violated the Amendment by assigning students on the basis of race when such assignments were not necessary to remedy a federal constitutional violation. *See* Brief for Bustop, Inc., 1-18. We do not reach this contention. **Crawford III**, 458 U.S. at 535, Fn. 11.

Notably, in that case Bustop, Inc. had taken a position in opposition to the busing order of the Superior Court, which the Los Angeles school board also was seeking to overturn. So the situation there differed from that which arose when the parent objections were raised to student assignments on the basis of race by the Charlotte-Mecklenburg school board under the purported authority of the 1971 **Swann** class action. It upheld its racially discriminatory assignments, and was joined in the following case by the **Swann** plaintiffs in opposing termination of the authority to continue them indefinitely.

Belk v. Charlotte-Mecklenburg Board of Education, Docket No. 99-2389, was rendered by the United States Court of Appeals for the Fourth Circuit, sitting *en banc*, on September 21, 2001. Pages referred to below are from its multiple opinions published on the internet at www.ca4.uscourts.gov at that time. (*Also see* ___ F.3d___.)

The Court, in its ruling, terminated court jurisdiction over the Charlotte-Mecklenburg Schools (CMS):

> Unitary status having been achieved, the judgment of the district court vacating and dissolving all prior injunctive orders and decrees is affirmed. The Board is to operate the school system without the strictures of these decrees no later than the 2002-2003 school year. *Id.* at 6,7 (*also see* ___ F.3d at ___).

The majority opinion, in rendering that judgment, sustained the district court's finding that CMS had achieved unitary status in all the **Green** categories, and notably "the most critical Green factor" of student assignment:

> In sum, the district court's findings on student assignment are "plausible in light of the record viewed in its entirety." **Anderson**, 470 U.S. at 573. The dual system of student assignment in CMS has been eradicated "to the extent practicable." **Dowell**, U.S. at 250... *Id.* at 29 (*also see* ___ F.3d at ___).

In arriving at its judgment, the Fourth Circuit provided a citation-guide available to parents and their counsel elsewhere seeking to restore local control after lengthy court supervision:

> In undertaking a unitary status inquiry, a court must ask "whether the Board ha(s) complied in good faith with the desegregation decree since it was entered, and whether the vestiges of past disrimination ha(ve) been eliminated to the extent practicable." **Board of Educ. v. Dowell**, 498 U.S. 237,249-50 (1991). Implicit in the Supreme Court's use of the word "practicable" is a reasonable limit on the duration of... federal supervision. **Coalition to Save Our Children v. State Bd. of Educ.**, 90 F.3d 752,760 (3d Cir. 1996); *see also* **Dowell**, 498 U.S. at 247 ("From the very first, federal supervision of local school systems was intended as a temporary measure to remedy past discrimination.") Hence, the goals of a desegregation order not only encompass a remedy for the violation, but also prompt restoration of local control. *See* **Freeman**, 503 U.S. at 490 (Returning schools to the control of local authorities at the earliest practicable date is essential to restore their true acountability in our

> governmental system... Where control lies, so does accountability."); **Milliken I**, 418 U.S. 741-742 ("No single tradition in public education is more deeply rooted than local control over the operation of schools; local automony has long been thought essential both to the maintenance of community concern and support for public schools and to quality of the educational process."). *Id.* at 17 (*also see* ___ F.3d at ___).

The success of the parents in the CMS system in restoring local control, under the above guidelines, supports challenges by other parents toward local control. This is particularly so as to the single (**Green**) factor of student assignment, as achieved in **Freeman**. The CMS parent achievement of release from court juridiction was remarkable in view of the opposition posed by their school board in conjunction with the **Swann** plaintiffs.

The parents also won a temporary victory when the district court awarded their attorneys fees from CMS for achieving a judicial declaration of unitary status for that school system. But a Fourth Circuit majority disallowed those fees over a three-judge dissent, which expressed the following concern on December 14, 2001:

> ...Should another case like this arise where the original plaintiffs and the school board are content to let the desegregation order remain in place long after the dual system has been dismantled, parents demanding a return of local control will be helpless. **Belk**, *supra*, Docket No. 992389R2.P, p.8 (*see also* ___F.3d at ___).

But parents in other districts must not let this adverse aspect, of a ruling which invokes **Dowell** and **Freeman** as governing these cases, stop the efforts by them and their counsel to return local control.

The author and the Groundswell parents faced the same odds upon the retention of jurisdiction by the **Carlin** Court, with the support of the school board and original plaintiffs, lasting a total of twenty years. But with each year of continuing court jurisdiction elsewhere, the mandate of **Freeman** to relinquish jurisdiction becomes stronger, as does the federalism argument asserted in that case.

The Conclusion of this *Handbook* explores innovative means available to parents toward the restoration of local control of the public education of their children, particularly as to their school assignments.

CONCLUSION

On January 15, 1991 the parents in Oklahoma City welcomed the restoration of local control of the public education of their children, decreed in their school district by the Supreme Court, with these words:

> (N)ecessary concern for the important values of local control of public school systems dictates that a federal court's regulatory control of such systems not extend beyond the time required to remedy the effects of past intentional discrimination. **Board of Ed. of Oklahoma City v. Dowell**. 498 U.S. 237,247-248.

This decision was also welcomed by the thousands of parents in the hundreds of public school systems remaining under the regulatory control of federal courts in desegregation class actions. But shortly, on January 22, 1991, a headline in *The Los Angeles Daily Journal*, "School Officials Nationwide React Cautiously to Desegregation Ruling," accurately anticipated that officials in those school districts would not readily follow the **Dowell** dictate to gain release from court control:

> "School districts will wait until there is a case that is more definitive," said Michael D. Simpson, staff counsel for the National Education Association.

A definitive case came on March 31, 1992 when parents in DeKalb County, Georgia, welcomed high court restoration of local control as to the public school assignments of their children, decreed in **Freeman v. Pitts**. Its decree reiterated that court supervision in such actions be returned to local control "at the earliest practicable date." 503 U.S. at 489.

Groundswell parents in San Diego welcomed **Freeman** by immediately moving on April 6, 1992 to terminate the **Carlin** Court jurisdiction and return San Diego schools to local control. But the San Diego Board, rather than emulate the school boards in **Dowell** and **Freeman**, vigorously joined the **Carlin** plaintiffs in opposing termination of court jurisdiction. The entire burden of restoring local control in San Diego, as related in Challenges Four and Five, was thereby placed upon the

Groundswell Intervenors. On July 1, 1998, their reliance upon **Dowell** and **Freeman** proved well founded when the Court of Appeal, in ending court jurisdiction, cited the emphasis in both those decisions of returning local control. **Board of Education v. Superior Court**, 61 Cal.App.4th 411,416,419.

The actions of the Defendant San Diego Board in joining the effort of **Carlin** Plaintiffs to indefinitely prolong court jurisdiction were not aberrant. For parents in the Charlotte-Mecklenburg school system saw their school board, defendant in **Swann v. Charlotte-Mecklenburg Board of Education** (1971), join with the **Swann** plaintiffs in opposing their effort to restore local control. They finally regained local control of the public education of their children on September 21, 2001. The Fourth Circuit U.S. Court of Appeals decreed it in **Belk v. Charlotte-Mecklenburg Board of Education**, with the guideline to local control quoted in foregoing Challenge Six, pp.82-83, citing both **Dowell** and **Freeman**.

Earlier, the Center for Equal Opportunity (CEO) publicized a caseload list, compiled March 1997 by the United States Department of Justice, of school desegregation cases in hundreds of school districts remaining under court jurisdiction. In a publication, *Civil Rights News*, CEO disclosed a letter written by it on October 5, 1998 to federal judges whose jurisdictions included school districts under desegregation orders. The letter noted in view of recent Supreme Court decisions that a review of the status of some cases had reportedly been undertaken by some judges to ascertain whether a continued judicial role (in some cases over 20 years) exceeded their Article III authority. It suggested the judges should ask the parties in these cases "to show cause why these school districts should not be declared unitary, the cases dismissed, full authority for making educational decisions returned to the local school boards, and the federal judicial role to end."

Such an order to show cause directed to the plaintiffs and defendant school boards is urgently needed by parents continuously lacking a democratic voice in such school districts. But experience shows they must provide the impetus for gaining such a review. Groundswell parents did so by obtaining counsel, necessarily *pro bono*, and presenting their vital interests, initially as *amici curiae*, per Appendix. Such a course is likely available to other similarly dedicated parents, at least as to an *amici* presentation, by way of counsel to whom "*pro bono* service is a hallmark of the legal profession." *See ABA Journal*, Feb. 1998, "President's Message."

In particular, a review as to the **Green** factor of student assignment could be presented by parents, as *amici curiae*, who are real parties in interest as to that factor. Official records of the trial courts and the school districts alone will warrant such presentations where they reflect a situation similar to that presented by former Solicitor General Lee (Challenge 3, pp.47-51) for release of court jurisdiction in that category in **Freeman**:

> ...Rex E. Lee, of Provo, Utah, argued before the Supreme Court on behalf of DCSS. According to Lee, DeKalb County grew rapidly after the issuance of the 1969 order to desegregate. Since that time, he said, the percentage of black students in the school population increased from 5 to 50 percent. And, he continued, the district court concluded it was the shift in population that caused the resegregation, not any action taken by DCSS....
>
> The approach Lee urged upon the court was for it to look at what caused the segregation in question. If you do that, he said, **Pasadena**... disposes of both issues in this case. First, he said, the demographic shifts are not attributable to DCSS, and thus should not reflect upon its unitary status. Second, the non-attainment of one factor in **Pasadena** did not require an overall change in the other factors.
>
> Lee shifted gears and closed with a discussion of federalism and the efficient allocation of resources. Under **Dowell**, he said, school systems should be run by local governing bodies, and not federal courts. For 22 years, DCSS has been trying to obey the law, but now, due to circumstances beyond its control, it is being told it will have to continue under court supervision for an indefinite length of time. Under the Eleventh Circuit's opinion, Lee noted, his clients are looking to more busing and radical gerry-mandering....

Amici curiae parents could similarly argue that demographic shifts should not reflect upon the unitary status of the student assignment **Green** factor when all that is practicable has been done to attain that status. *Amici* could further similarly argue the concept of federalism requires the end of court supervision as to student assignment. This concept was advanced by the author initially in an *amici* brief (Appendix) as to the **Carlin** class action and later in his books to other class actions.

In addition, *Amici* can argue the separate interest of parents opposed to the racial discrimination of their children in their school assignments in the ongoing "desegregation" supervisions. History teaches that *amici curiae* presentations have been very effective where an interest against racial discrimination is not otherwise represented in a proceeding before the court. *See* dictum in **Jackson v. Pasadena City School District** (1963), reviewed in Note, 51 *Cal.L.Review* 810).

Another precedent supports appointment of an attorney as *amicus curiae* in a case where an important interest against race discrimination is otherwise unrepresented.

The maintenance of a form of racial discrimination prompted the judicial appointment of an *amicus curiae* in **Bob Jones University v. United States**, 456 U.S. 922 (1982). The interests to be advanced by an *amicus* in these "desegregation" class actions may be compared to those against racial discrimination in **Bob Jones University v. United States**, 461 U.S. 574 (1983). Being unrepresented, those interests were presented by the appointed *amicus* in that case.

Bob Jones University, a private religious university, had a policy prohibiting interracial dating and marriage by its white and black students. This was racially discriminatory, according to Internal Revenue Service policy, which formed the basis for denying a claimed tax exempt status. *Id.* at 581.

The Court found the university policy was a form of racial discrimination (reportedly since discontinued), and upheld *amicus*' position in support of the judgment below finding the IRS policy was properly applied to Bob Jones University. *Id.* at 605.

In the course of its ruling, the Supreme Court emphasized that *there is a national policy against racial discrimination in education, and that the government has a fundamental, overriding interest in eradicating it. Id.* at 593,604.

APPENDIX

Elmer Enstrom, Jr.
890 Knob Hill Dr.; P. O. Box 723
Julian, California 92036
Telephone: (714) 765-0520

F I L E D Robert D. Zumwalt, Clerk
OCT 10 1980
BY S. TALBOTT DEPUTY

Attorney for Groundswell, et al., Applicants-Movants to appear and file brief as Interested Persons and Amici Curiae

SUPERIOR COURT OF CALIFORNIA, COUNTY OF SAN DIEGO

KARI CARLIN, et al.,
Plaintiffs,
v.
BOARD OF EDUCATION, SAN DIEGO UNIFIED SCHOOL DISTRICT,
Defendant.

CASE NO 303800

APPLICATION OF GROUNDSWELL, LARRY K. LESTER, STEPHEN E. LESTER, AND CHRISTINA MARIE LESTER FOR LEAVE TO APPEAR AND FILE A BRIEF, AS INTERESTED PERSONS AND AS AMICI CURIAE, IN OPPOSITION TO PLAINTIFFS' PROPOSED FINDINGS OF FACT, CONCLUSIONS OF LAW AND ORDER APPOINTING SPECIAL MASTER WITH POWER TO MAKE MANDATORY PUPIL ASSIGNMENTS ON THE BASIS OF THEIR RACE TO PARTICULAR SCHOOLS IN THE SAN DIEGO UNIFIED SCHOOL DISTRICT; ORDER.

DECLARATION OF LARRY K. LESTER IN SUPPORT OF APPLICATION TO APPEAR AND FILE BRIEF, AS INTERESTED PERSONS AND AS AMICI CURIAE.

BRIEF OF GROUNDSWELL, ET AL., AS INTERESTED PERSONS AND AS AMICI CURIAE, IN OPPOSITION TO PLAINTIFFS' PROPOSED FINDINGS OF FACT, CONCLUSIONS OF LAW AND ORDER APPOINTING SPECIAL MASTER WITH POWER TO MAKE MANDATORY PUPIL ASSIGNMENTS ON THE BASIS OF THEIR RACE TO PARTICULAR SCHOOLS IN THE SAN DIEGO UNIFIED SCHOOL DISTRICT.

APPLICATION OF GROUNDSWELL, LARRY K. LESTER, STEPHEN E. LESTER, AND CHRISTINA MARIE LESTER FOR LEAVE TO APPEAR AND FILE A BRIEF, AS INTERESTED PERSONS AND AS AMICI CURIAE IN OPPOSITION TO PLAINTIFFS' PROPOSED FINDINGS OF FACT, CONCLUSIONS OF LAW AND ORDER APPOINTING SPECIAL MASTER WITH POWER TO MAKE MANDATORY PUPIL ASSIGNMENTS ON THE BASIS OF THEIR RACE TO PARTICULAR SCHOOLS IN THE SAN DIEGO UNIFIED SCHOOL DISTRICT

Groundswell, an unincorporated association of persons, which includes parents, taxpayers and electors residing in the San Diego Unified School District (SDUSD), Larry K. Lester, a taxpayer-parent-elector residing in the SDUSD, his son Stephen E. Lester, a resident and attendee of his neighborhood SDUSD school at times pertinent herein, and his daughter, Christina Marie Lester, a ninth grade attendee of her neighborhood SDUSD school, respectfully apply and move to appear and to file the annexed brief, and to argue orally in support thereof, as Interested Persons and as Amici Curiae, under Section 7(a), Article I of the California Constitution, as amended November 6, 1979 (Proposition 1 - annexed as appendix hereto) and the rules of this Court.

Applicants Groundswell, Larry K. Lester and Stephen E. Lester appeared as Amici Curiae at the evaluation hearings held pursuant to the order of July 27, 1978, on June 25, 26, 28 and July 2 and 3, 1979, and presented oral and written argument in opposition to the effort by plaintiffs at said hearings to introduce mandatory assignments of pupils, because of their race, into the SDUSD integration plan.

On October 2, 1979, this Court filed its Order Re Integration Plan 1979-82 without requiring mandatory pupil assignments. On November 6, 1979, the electors of the state amended the California Constitution by the enactment of Proposition 1, and the Court is asked to take judicial notice of the vote in the SDUSD favoring Proposition 1. On November 28, 1979, plaintiffs filed notice of appeal from aforesaid October 2, 1979, order.

On September 19, 1980, applicants Groundswell, Larry K. Lester and Stephen E. Lester, with permission of the Court of Appeal, Fourth Appellate District, appeared in this case on the appeal from said order of October 2, 1979, being 4 Civil No. 22051, and filed a brief, as Interested Persons and as Amici Curiae, in support of their position, and the position of the Respondent Board of Education, SDUSD, opposing mandatory pupil assignments. The Court is asked to take judicial notice of such filing.

Plaintiffs, by an application filed October 3, 1980, request the Court to issue the following order:

> "Defendant school district shall cooperate with a court-appointed Special Master, experienced in integrating schools, to immediately formulate a comprehensive desegregation plan which will eliminate segregated schools in San Diego and thus meet the mandate of Crawford. Part of the plan to be developed by the Special Master shall be designed to maximize classroom integration in every school in the District."

Plaintiffs also propose findings of fact and conclusions of law in support of such an order. Thereby, although not saying so directly, they again seek to inject the element of mandatory pupil assignments into the SDUSD integration plan to alleviate "segregation" not found to be unconstitutional under the United States Constitution. Such assignments would therefore be in violation of, and raise the issue of the constitutionality of, Proposition 1.

3

By their proposals, in a proceeding between only themselves and the defendant Board, plaintiffs seek affirmative "relief" which would be accomplished by a special master and would adversely affect movants and others similarly situated and affected. Involuntary student assignees, and their parents, opposed to their being the objects of a busing draft, on account of their race, completely controlled and operated by a special master, even more so than before, are the real parties in interest in this proceeding, and face the loss of rights they alone can best decry.

Movants' interests and their stake in the outcome of plaintiffs' present proposals are such as to entitle them to make an Amici Curiae presentation. In addition, the passage of Proposition 1 gives them the right to appear and make a presentation as Interested Persons--parents, students, taxpayers and electors--who would be affected adversely by plaintiffs' proposed findings of fact, conclusions of law and order.

Wherefore, movants respectfully request that their application to appear, and to file the attached brief, as Interested Persons and as Amici Curiae, and to argue orally in support of their position, be granted.

DATED: October 10, 1980

Respectfully submitted,

/S/
ELMER ENSTROM, JR., ESQ.,
Attorney for Applicants-Movants
Groundswell, Larry K. Lester,
Stephen E. Lester and Christina
Marie Lester

ORDER

OCT 10 1980

So ordered, this ____ day of October, 1980.

LOUIS M. WELSH
JUDGE OF THE SUPERIOR COURT

4

Elmer Enstrom, Jr.
890 Knob Hill Dr.; P.O.Box 723
Julian, California 92036
(714) 765-0520

Attorney for Groundswell, et al.,
as Interested Persons and
as Amici Curiae

SUPERIOR COURT OF CALIFORNIA, COUNTY OF SAN DIEGO

KARI CARLIN, et al., Plaintiffs, v. BOARD OF EDUCATION, SAN DIEGO UNIFIED SCHOOL DISTRICT, Defendant.	CASE NO. 303800 DECLARATION OF LARRY K. LESTER IN SUPPORT OF APPLICATION TO APPEAR AND FILE BRIEF, AS INTERESTED PERSONS AND AS AMICI CURIAE

I, LARRY K. LESTER, under penalty of perjury, declare:

1. I reside in San Diego County, California, within the San Diego Unified School District (hereinafter referred to as "SDUSD") with my wife and children, including my son Stephen E. Lester and my daughter, Christina Marie Lester, who is in the ninth grade and presently attends her neighborhood school in the SDUSD. I pay taxes toward the support of the SDUSD. I, my wife and my children are opposed to the mandatory assignments of my daughter, and other public school children similarly situated and affected, because of their race, to particular schools (forced busing) in the SDUSD.

2. I am President of Groundswell. Groundswell is an

unincorporated association of persons residing in California, including persons I am informed and believe, and therefore allege, are parents, taxpayers and electors residing in the SDUSD. Groundswell was organized in 1977, and its objectives include opposing mandatory assignments of public school students, because of their race, to particular public schools.

3.In support of the objectives of Groundswell, I and other members of Groundswell, during the period from about June 1, 1977, to about October 1, 1977, gathered the signatures of about 22,300 persons from all parts of California, including the SDUSD, in support of an amendment to the United States Constitution called the "Neighborhood Schools Amendment," which includes a provision that no student be compelled to attend a public school other than the one nearest the residence of such student.

4. I circulated many of aforesaid petitions and talked with thousands of the signers at the respective times they signed said petitions, and with many of them, including some of their children, since that time. Many of the petitioners advised me that they had children attending public schools in the SDUSD. Many of the petitioning parents advised me that they and their children opposed the forced busing of their children. Many of the children advised me that they opposed being bused away from their neighborhood schools. Many of the petitioners advised me that they were aware of the <u>Crawford</u> v. <u>Board of Education</u> decision (17 Cal.3d 280) rendered in 1976, and made statements to the effect that they did not believe their interests had been represented in that proceeding. I do not believe that my interests and those of my children, and other public school parents and

2

children similarly situated and affected, were represented in the course of the proceedings leading to said Crawford decision.

5. I have talked with residents of the Los Angeles Unified School District, as well as with members of the governing board of said district, about aforesaid Crawford decision. I am informed and believe, and therefore allege, that requests were made by constituents of the governing board of said district that it appeal aforesaid Crawford decision to the United States Supreme Court, and that a majority of said board refused to do so.

6. I observed the actions taking place concerning the trial of this case, which was concluded in 1977, as closely as my employment and obligations to my family permitted, and read accounts pertaining to same, as well as attending events in connection therewith, including defendant Board meetings. At a number of these Board meeting, I, and other persons, made requests of SDUSD Board members of positions they should take in our behalf as parents opposed to forced busing whose children were attending SDUSD schools, in connection with this suit, which were not acted upon by the defendant Board.

7. I also discussed at my home and at other places on numerous occasions in 1977, the events taking place in this lawsuit and at SDUSD board meetings, with numerous persons, including some who, with me, formed "Groundswell." It was the consensus of opinion at such discussions that we needed separate legal representation of our views concerning the lawsuit, but that we would be financially unable to pay the attorneys fees required for such representation. The obligations for attorneys fees which were reported at that time concerning a group in Los Angeles

called "Bustop" trying to present similar views opposing forced busing in court were brought out in the course of these discussions.

8. Following these discussions, I continuously explored the possibility of obtaining legal representation, which included conversations with attorneys. One attorney advised me that he did not have the expertise to undertake such representation. I also was unsuccessful in the spring of 1978 in having another attorney see if our representation could be undertaken at that time by an organization on a public interest basis without attorneys fees. It was not until the spring of 1979 that I and other members of Groundswell were successful in having our representation in this case undertaken by Elmer Enstrom, Jr., our present counsel, on a pro bono publico basis that would not obligate us for attorneys fees.

9. I, my wife, and our children, have been, and are financially unable to pay attorneys fees for representation in a case of this magnitude.

10. In support of the objectives of Groundswell, I and other members of Groundswell participated in a committee supporting passage of Proposition 1, which I believe and they believe, according to my information and belief, is a legislatively proposed constitutional amendment designed to prevent forced busing under aforesaid Crawford decision. I, and the other Groundswell members participating in this committee, according to my information and belief, voted for the passage of Proposition 1 on November 6, 1979.

11. I am informed and believe and therefore allege that there has been no finding in this case that the "segregation" in the SDUSD violates the United States Constitution.

4

12. I, my wife, my son Stephen E. Lester, my daughter Christina Marie Lester, Groundswell and its members, and other persons similarly situated and affected as parents, students, taxpayers, and electors residing in the SDUSD, have an interest, not separately represented herein, in upholding the constitutionality of Proposition 1.

Executed this 10th day of October, 1980, at San Diego, California.

/S/

Larry K. Lester, Declarant

5

SUPERIOR COURT OF CALIFORNIA, COUNTY OF SAN DIEGO

KARI CARLIN, et al., Plaintiffs, v. BOARD OF EDUCATION, SAN DIEGO UNIFIED SCHOOL DISTRICT, Defendant.	)	CASE NO. 303800

BRIEF OF GROUNDSWELL, ET AL., AS INTERESTED PERSONS AND AS AMICI CURIAE, IN OPPOSITION TO PLAINTIFFS' PROPOSED FINDINGS OF FACT, CONCLUSIONS OF LAW AND ORDER APPOINTING SPECIAL MASTER WITH POWER TO MAKE MANDATORY PUPIL ASSIGNMENTS ON THE BASIS OF THEIR RACE TO PARTICULAR SCHOOLS IN THE SAN DIEGO UNIFIED SCHOOL DISTRICT

ELMER ENSTROM, JR., ESQ.
Attorney at Law
890 Knob Hill Drive
Post Office Box 723
Julian, California 92036
Phone (714) 765-0520

Attorney for Groundswell,
Larry K. Lester,
Stephen E. Lester and
Christina Marie Lester

POINTS AND AUTHORITIES

I

PLAINTIFFS SEEK TO IMPOSE OBLIGATIONS UPON DEFENDANT WHICH WOULD IMPACT ADVERSELY UPON UNJOINED INTERESTED PERSONS, IN VIOLATION OF THE CALIFORNIA CONSTITUTION, AS AMENDED ON NOVEMBER 6, 1979

The defendant is administering an all voluntary integration plan, which was approved by the trial court. Plaintiffs seek by their proposal to have introduced, by a "master", mandatory assignments of unjoined persons, on account of their race, to particular schools on authority of Crawford v. Board of Education (1976) 17 Cal. 3d 280.

Such mandatory assignments are sought on the basis of a finding that some of the schools in the SDUSD are "segregated" in terms of the proportion of minority students attending such schools in relation to white attendance, without regard as to how such racial attendance has come about.

However, an order based on such a finding of de facto segregation would impose upon defendant obligations which exceed those required by federal decisions construing the Equal Protection Clause of the 14th Amendment. As Chief Justice Burger said in Swann (402 U.S. at 28): "Absent a constitutional violation there would be no basis for judicially ordering assignments of students on a racial basis."

Justice Powell noted in the decisive opinion in University of California Regents v. Bakke (1977), 438 U.S. 265 at 307:

> "We have never approved a classification that aids persons perceived as members of relatively victimized groups at the expense of other innocent individuals in the absence of judicial, legislative, or administrative

2

findings of constitutional or statutory violations."

On November 6, 1979, Subdivision (a) of Section 7 of Article I of the California Constitution was amended to provide in part as follows:

"(a) A person may not be deprived of life, liberty, or property without due process of law or denied equal protection of the laws; provided, that nothing contained herein or elsewhere in this Constitution imposes upon the State of California or any public entity, board, or official any obligations or responsibilities which exceed those imposed by the Equal Protection Clause of the 14th Amendment to the United States Constitution with respect to the use of pupil school assignment or pupil transportation. In enforcing this subdivision or any other provision of this Constitution, no court of this state may impose upon the State of California or any public entity, board, or official any obligation or responsibility with respect to the use of pupil school assignment or pupil transportation, (1) except to remedy a specific violation by such party that would also constitute a violation of the Equal Protection Clause of the 14th Amendment to the United States Constitution, and (2) unless a federal court would be permitted under federal decisional law to impose that obligation or responsibility upon such party to remedy the specific violation of the Equal Protection Clause of the 14th Amendment of the United States Constitution..."

The California and federal standards for equal protection

had been held by California courts to be substantially the same. County of Los Angeles v. Southern Cal. Tel. Co. (1948), 32 Cal.2d 378, 389; Sail'er Inn, Inc. v. Kirby (1971), 5 Cal.3d 1, 15-16, Fn. 13. Crawford departed from the federal standard without adequate consideration of the position of those children and their parents who would suffer under the new standard. Those to be subjected to busing were not parties in Crawford, nor had their interests been represented in Jackson v. Pasadena City School Dist. (1963) 59 Cal.2d 876, upon which Crawford so heavily relies.

Now, such interested persons as these movants are guaranteed the right to be heard on their objections to the injection of forced busing into this case by the following provision of Section 7(a) of Article I:

> "Except as may be precluded by the Constitution of the United States, every existing judgment, decree, writ, or other order of a court of this state, whenever rendered, which includes provisions regarding pupil school assignment or pupil transportation, or which requires a plan including any such provisions shall, upon application to a court having jurisdiction by any interested person, be modified to conform to the provisions of this subdivision as amended, as applied to the facts which exist at the time of such modification." (Emphasis added.)

To order mandatory pupil assignments in this case would be to deny the people of California the power to amend their Constitution, whether carried out by the Board or a Special Master.

Article I, Section 1, of the California Constitution provides:

> "All people are by nature free and independent and have

4

inalienable rights. Among these are enjoying and defending life and liberty, acquiring, possessing, and protecting property, and pursuing and obtaining safety, happiness, and privacy."

And Section 24 provides: "...This declarationof rights may not be construed to impair or deny others retained by the people."

The people have the power to amend their Constitution, as proposed by a two-thirds majority of their Legislature, to correct an interpretation which has no support in the holdings of the highest federal court, and which rests upon a sociological basis.

Since plaintiffs seek to introduce race discrimination by governmental authority into a nondiscriminatory voluntary integration plan, they propose conduct obviously more culpable than the "nonobvious" involvement of the State in private racially discriminatory conduct disallowed in Mulkey v. Reitman (1966), 64 Cal.2d 529. Aff'd Reitman v. Mulkey (1967), 387 U.S. 369.

The plaintiffs are specifically and validly enjoined by the California Constitution, as amended by Proposition 1, from obtaining from a master the mandatory pupil assignments sought by their proposal.

5

II

THE ADDITIONAL AFFIRMATIVE RELIEF SOUGHT AGAINST UNJOINED THIRD PARTIES SHOULD BE DENIED

By their request appellants seek to have authority placed in a master to take additional affirmative action, including the mandatory busing of unjoined students because of their race.

Plaintiffs have been given notice that these applicants-movants object to such discriminatory affirmative action which would injure and adversely affect their interests.

In Sierra Club, Inc. v. California Coastal Com. (1979), 95 Cal.App.3d 495, plaintiff Sierra Club sought by mandamus to have the Coastal Commission and a regional commission ordered to set aside a permit to a developer of a real estate project. Because the plaintiff failed to name the developer as a party within 60 days of the final decisions of the commissions, the court ordered dismissal of the action. The court pointed out that for reasons of equity and convenience it should not proceed with that case where it determined an "indispensable" party was absent and could not be joined. 95 Cal.App.3d at 500.

Where a plaintiff seeks some other type of affirmative relief which, if granted, would injure or affect the interest of a third person not joined, that third person is an indispensable party. Bank of California v. Superior Court (1940), 16 Cal.2d 516 at 522.

Section 389, California Code of Civil Procedure, requires the joinder of "(a) A person who is subject to service of process and whose joinder will not deprive the court of jurisdiction over the subject matter of the action...if (1) in his absence

6

complete relief cannot be accorded among those already parties or (2) he claims an interest relating to the subject of the action and is so situated that the disposition of the action in his absence may (i) as a practical matter impair or impede his ability to protect that interest..."

Only the children to be bused because of their race have the ability to fully protect their interest against being bused! Only they can invoke the protection due them under the Due Process Clause of the 14th Amendment, which provides that no State shall deprive any person of life, liberty or property, without due process of law. See Pierce v. Society of Sisters (1925), 268 U.S. 510, 535.

Only the parents whose children are to be bused because of their race have the ability to fully protect their interest against having their children bused! Only they can invoke the protection due them under the Due Process Clause to prevent the State from unreasonably interfering with their liberty to direct the upbringing and education of their children. See Pierce v. Society of Sisters, supra, and Wisconsin v. Yoder (1972), 406 U.S. 205.

As thistrial court pointed out in its Memorandum Decision and Order on March 9, 1977, while a state may grant its citizens greater rights than those afforded under the federal Constitution, it may do so only so long as it does not result in a denial of a federal right.

To quote this Court:

"As our State Supreme Court stated in the recent case of Serrano v. Priest, 18 Cal.3d 728, 765 (12/30/76), '(I)n the area of fundamental civil liberties...we sit as a court of last resort, subject only to the qualifications that our interpretations may not restrict the guarantees accorded the national citizenry under the federal charter.'"

The personal interests threatened by the affirmative action sought by the plaintiffs have long been considered deserving of the most careful consideration. The busing here sought especially requires strict scrutiny because it would introduce race discrimination by governmental force into an integration plan heretofore free from such state action. And it can't receive such scrutiny in the absence of the real parties in interest entitled to urge it. See Bakke v. Regents of University of California (1976), 18 Cal.3d 34, 49; and University of California Regents v. Bakke (1977), 438 U.S. 265, 299.

The Sierra Club case goes on to say (95 Cal.App.3d at 500) that in the absence of an indispensable party the court will still have the power to render a decision as to the parties before it which will stand. But under the Bank of California decision, any attempt to secure additional affirmative relief, such as the forced busing sought here, injuring and affecting the interests of unjoined parties, is futile and is beyond the jurisdiction of the court. 16 Cal.2d at 522.

III

PLAINTIFFS SEEK TO SUBJECT OBJECTING STUDENTS TO DISCRIMINATION ON THE GROUND OF RACE UNDER A PROGRAM RECEIVING FEDERAL FINANCIAL ASSISTANCE, IN VIOLATION OF THE CIVIL RIGHTS ACT OF 1964

Section 601 of Title VI of the Civil Rights Act of 1964 (42 U.S.C.A. 2000d) provides:

> "No person in the United States shall, on the ground of race, color, or national origin, be excluded from participation in, be denied the benefits of, or be subjected to discrimination under any program or activity receiving Federal financial assistance."

In University of California Regents v. Bakke, supra, Justice Stevens, speaking also for three other justices, would have granted Bakke relief, by ordering his admission to U. C. Davis under the foregoing provision. 438 U.S. at 421. SDUSD, like Davis, receives Federal financial assistance.

The contention by the University of California Regents in the foregoing case that such relief could not be sought and obtained by a private litigant under aforesaid Act is untenable in view of the decision reached in Cannon v. University of Chicago (1979), 441 U.S. 677, 99 S.Ct. 1946. Justice Stevens, now speaking for a majority, in a case by a nurse alleging discrimination on account of her sex, in violation of Sec. 901(a) of Title of the Education Amendments of 1972, in her effort to enter a college receiving Federal assistance, said at 99 S.Ct. 1968:

> "We therefore conclude that petitioner may maintain her lawsuit, despite the absence of any express authorization for it in the statute."

9

In Bakke v. Regents of University of California, supra, the California Supreme Court upheld the objections of Bakke that the actions excluding him from U. C. Davis' medical school, solely on account of his Caucasian race, violated his constitutional rights under the Equal Protection Clause of the 14th Amendment.

Upon appeal to the U. S. Supreme Court, Justice Powell, in the decisive opinion in University of California Regents v. Bakke, supra, held that the use of explicit racial classification barring Bakke from admission violated the Equal Protection Clause, although the California court erred in enjoining Davis from ever considering the race of an applicant in a properly devised admissions program. Justice Powell noted significantly that the Petitioner University Regents had failed to make a showing of constitutional or statutory violations which could be said to give the State an interest in preferring members of purportedly injured groups at the expense of innocent individuals like Bakke. 438 U.S. at 308-309.

In United Steelworkers, Etc. v. Weber (1979), 441 U.S. 193, 99 S.Ct. 2721, Weber charged that a Kaiser-United Steelworkers affirmative action plan discriminated against him and similarly situated white employees at Kaiser's plant in Louisiana. The plan provided for the selection of a specified number of black and white employees in proportion to the population of the area to be selected for a craft training program. It had the effect of admitting into the training program, before Weber and other whites similarly situated, blacks with less seniority than the complaining whites.

The Supreme Court refused to invalidate the plan because the majority felt the legislative history showed the legislators did not intend to limit traditional business freedom to such a degree as to prohibit an all voluntary plan such as this one. The decision was limited to the facts of the case, the Court stating at 99 S.Ct. 2730: "We need not today define in detail the line of demarcation between permissible and impermissible affirmative action plans." (443 U.S. at 208.)

In holding that the prohibition in Title VII of the Civil Rights Act (42 U.S.C.A. 2000e-2(a,d)) against racial discrimination in employment did not condemn the plan before it in Weber, the Court advised that since the plan was adopted voluntarily, it was not concerned with what Title VII requires or with what a court might order to remedy a past proven violation of the Act.

The narrow Weber holding does not diminish the validity of the objections of these innocent students under Title VI to the racially discriminatory busing which plaintiffs propose be imposed upon them. And their objections, which have been made known to plaintiffs are entitled to be considered and should be sustained.

11

IV

PLAINTIFFS SEEK STATE ACTION DISCRIMINATING AGAINST UNJOINED INTERESTED PERSONS, BECAUSE OF THEIR RACE, IN VIOLATION OF THE EQUAL PROTECTION CLAUSE OF THE FOURTEENTH AMENDMENT

In Brown v. Board of Education (Brown I) (1954), the issues arising from the pleadings fairly may be said to have called only for considering the complaints of black children that they were discriminated against by the laws of Kansas and three other states. In each case, the black complainants were segregated because of their race in public schools administered by the respondent school authorities under the laws of their respective states.

The Supreme Court, in deciding these cases between the parties before it, held that the complaining black students, and others similarly situated were, by reason of the segregation complained of, deprived of equal protection of the laws guaranteed by the 14th Amendment of the United States Constitution, which provides in pertinent part: "(N)or shall any State...deny to any person within its jurisdiction the equal protection of the laws."

The complainants in Brown I did not seek the busing of other children, on account of their race, to alleviate segregation. Therefore, the question of the denial of equal protection rights which would occur to those adversely affected by this form of reverse discrimination was not then considered.

In later suits, complainants continued to name only the allegedly offending governmental authorities, while broadening their claims to affirmative relief ultimately impacting upon persons not joined.

In Jackson v. Pasadena City School Dist., supra, the theory of

12

an additional duty of "affirmative integration" appears to have had its genesis in the briefs of amici curiae. See Note, 51 Cal. L.Rev. 810, 811, n.5 (1963). This became dictum in Jackson, which in turn has grown to become authority for affirmative integration by forced busing in a series of California cases, reaching its apex in Crawford, and leading to the present effort by appellants to interject mandatory, racially discriminatory, assignments of third persons into a nondiscriminatory integration plan.

The impact upon such third persons has been noted by Justice Powell in his concurring opinion in Austin Independent School District v. United States (1976), 429 U.S. 990 at 995, Fn. 7:

> "The individual interests at issue here are as personal and important as any in our society. They relate to the family, and to the concern of parents for the welfare and education of their children--especially those of tender age. Families share these interests wholly without regard to race, ethnic origin, or economic status. It also is to be remembered, in granting equitable relief, that a desegregation decree is unique in that its burden falls not upon the officials or private interests responsible for the offending action but, rather, upon innocent children and parents."

The burden referred to by Justice Powell has fallen, and is proposed to fall in the SDUSD, upon innocents solely by reason of their race, without their having had an opportunity to raise equal protection objections in the adversary sense which the American system of justice demands. In the absence of representa-

13

tion of interests paralleling their own in earlier cases, these Interested Persons necessarily must present original arguments.

These Interested Persons urge that the Color-Blind doctrine, enunciated by Justice Harlan I, in dissent in Plessy v. Ferguson (1896), 163 U.S. 537, 559, prevents the busing of unjoined interested children because such busing is dependent solely upon an impermissible classification, namely, the race of said children. The Color-Blind doctrine, which these Interested Persons believe Brown I did, and should now, stand for, was restated by the late Chief Justice in The Memoirs of Earl Warren (1977; Doubleday) at pp. 287-288:

> "Again the Court was unanimous in its decision of May 31, 1955, (Brown II) reaffirming its earlier opinion of May 17, 1954, (Brown I) by asserting the fundamental principle that any kind of racial discrimination in public education is unconstitutional, and that all provisions of federal, state, or local law requiring or permitting such discrimination must yield to this principle." (Reference to Brown I and Brown II cases and underscoring added by Interested Persons.)

Racially discriminatory busing was introduced into Los Angeles schools as a result of the Crawford decision (referred to at p. 2 of this brief), even though it can be fairly asserted, movants believe, that the record shows L. A. schools had never been operated under a constitutional or statutory provision that mandated or permitted racial segregation in public education.

The judiciary's nonpublication rules do not permit citation of

14

certain authority for this proposition; however, the lack of reference to any such constitutional or statutory provisions in the Crawford decision is supportive of a claim that the Los Angeles schools did not operate under laws comparable to those considered in Brown I.

The judicial process by which such discrimination was introduced in Los Angeles, and is sought to be extended into the SDUSD, should be reexamined. Such an examination will show that the introduction of this discrimination was accomplished by means whereby the voices of those to be subjected to it were not adequately heard. A judicial review, in which the voices of the victims are heard, will in fairness require that the Crawford doctrine be discarded.

In any event, the Swann doctrine does not permit racially discriminatory busing of unjoined persons, in violation of their equal protection rights under the 14th Amendment, to remedy de facto segregation in the San Diego Unified School District.

15

V

PLAINTIFFS SEEK STATE ACTION INFRINGING UPON THE LIBERTY AND PRIVACY OF UNJOINED INTERESTED CHILDREN IN VIOLATION OF THE UNITED STATES CONSTITUTION

Children are not mere creatures of the State. Pierce v. Society of Sisters, supra, 268 U.S. at 535. They are protected by the United States Constitution from state action infringing upon their liberty and privacy.

The Due Process Clause of the 14th Amendment provides that no State shall deprive any person of life, liberty or property without due process of law.

The Warren Court, in construing a similarly worded clause in the 5th Amendment, in conjunction with that court's application of the Equal Protection Clause of the 14th Amendment in Brown I, pointed out in Bolling v. Sharpe (1954), 347 U.S. 497, that discrimination "may be so unjustifiable as to be violative of due process." The Court added: "Classifications based solely upon race must be scrutinized with particular care since they are contrary to our tradition and hence constitutionally suspect." 347 U.S. at 499.

The points in Bolling are pertinent because busing is here sought to be judicially imposed on a racially discriminatory basis which Californians voted to prohibit by Education Code 1009.6.

Such busing is also constitutionally suspect because of the judicial course taken towards its imposition. That course has been arbitrary and lacking in due process. It has included assuming the power to declare Sec. 1009.6 unconstitutional and to transform the dictum in Jackson that school boards take steps to alleviate racial imbalance into a constitutional doctrine forcing them to alleviate school segregation, regardless of its cause, by racially discriminatory means. And in each of the cases along this course, the children whose liberty and privacy is adversly affected by the judicially-imposed doctrine have not been present to object to making them pawns of court-ordered busing.

In addition, other judicial views concerning the rationale of Crawford, under which the objecting students' loss of rights has occurred, have been screened from public view by the California high court's Rules 976 and 977 prohibiting their publication and citation by counsel. This is inconsistent with the concept of a public trial from start, through the appeal process, to finish. Involuntary student assignees especially should have the benefit of public scrutiny of these unique judicial proceedings because of their defenselessness to actions affecting them taken in such proceedings.

No comparable prohibitions are imposed on lower court proceedings by the U. S. Supreme Court. Thus, had the wisdom of the dissent of Justice Harlan I in Plessy been contained in a federal Court of Appeals decision by him, it continuously would have remained available to all to cite and argue, as have many famous Second Circuit decisions by Judge Learned Hand. To preclude counsel from citing and arguing such decisions in support of their clients' positions denies the latter due process.

So long as a nondiscriminatory voluntary integration plan continues in the SDUSD, the goal of appellants of busing unjoined interested children is of somewhat the same concern as a draft law thought to be unconstitutional would be to persons before

17

they were classified or notified to report for induction. But when a busing draft begins to zero in on persons who oppose it, by a challenge to Proposition 1, due process demands they have an opportunity to raise and be heard upon the full range of their objections to it. The right to notice and opportunity to be heard must be granted at a meaningful time and in a meaningful manner. Armstrong v. Manzo (1965), 380 U.S. 545, 550, 552.

Goss v. Lopez (1975), 419 U.S. 565, arose out of widespread student unrest at an Ohio public high school in which nine students were suspended under an Ohio law permitting principals of public schools to suspend pupils for misconduct for up to ten days without appeal to higher school authority.

The Supreme Court held that the Due Process Clause required that, at the very minimum, students facing suspension (for as short as one day and not more than ten days) must be given some kind of notice and some kind of a hearing before suspension could be ordered. The Court pointed out that the case dealt only with short suspensions not exceeding 10 days and that more extensive discipline would likely require more formal procedures.

As stated by the high court in Bolling, supra, 347 U.S. at 497:

> "Although the Court has not assumed to define 'liberty' with any great precision, that term is not confined to mere freedom from bodily restraint. Liberty under law extends to the full range of conduct which the individual is free to pursue, and it cannot be restricted except for a proper governmental objective."

Busing of children away from their neighborhood schools

more seriously curbs the liberty of many more public school students over a longer period of time than was the case in Goss. The additional time they are governmentally required to spend on buses each day for an indefinite period also invades their privacy. See e.g., Roe v. Wade (1973), 410 U.S. 113, 152-153.

The State's interest in universal education is not free from a balancing of rights when it impinges upon such a fundamental right as the privacy of a child. Wisconsin v. Yoder, supra.

Justice Brandeis, in condemning by dissent a governmental invasion of privacy by a telephonic tap "search" in the criminal case of Olmstead v. United States (1928), 277 U.S. 438 at 478, underscored the value of the right of privacy:

> "The makers of our Constitution undertook to secure conditions favorable to the pursuit of happiness... They conferred, as against the Government, the right to be let alone--the most comprehensive of rights and the right most valued by civilized men."

Most fitting to the conclusion of this assertion of the federal due process and privacy rights of the unjoined interested children is the following portion of the Brandeis dissent:

> "Experience should teach us to be most on our guard to protect liberty when the Government's purposes are beneficent. Men born to freedom are naturally alert to repel invasion of their liberty by evil-minded rulers. The greatest dangers to liberty lurk in insidious encroachment by men of zeal, well-meaning, but without understanding." 277 U.S. at 479.

19

VI

PLAINTIFFS SEEK STATE ACTION INFRINGING UPON THE LIBERTY OF UNJOINED INTERESTED PARENTS, IN VIOLATION OF THE DUE PROCESS CLAUSE OF THE FOURTEENTH AMENDMENT

The Due Process Clause of the 14th Amendment of the United States Constitution prevents the states from unreasonably interfering with the liberty of parents to direct the upbringing and education of their children. Pierce v. Society of Sisters, supra, and Wisconsin v. Yoder, supra.

People v. Turner, 121 Cal.App.2d Sup. 861, App. Dismissed, 347 U.S. 972 (1954), held that the California compulsory education laws did not unreasonably interfere with the parents' liberty in that case.

However, the statute being construed in Turner must be distinguished from a superimposition thereupon of judicially-mandated busing. The statute was framed and enacted by representatives of the people in the traditional democratic process; judicially-superimposed busing is not so derived.

Not only does the judicial process lack the input by all interested persons, it does not have the flexibility of the legislative process for change. Nor is the judicial process subject to review by an independent branch of government.

Obviously, the mandatory transportation of children away from their neighborhood schools, among other things, decreases the ability of parents to care for the health and safety of their children. The parents' voices were not heard in the initial shaping of busing decrees relied upon by plaintiffs and unless heard now will continue to be muted while court-ordered busing of their children is sought to be instituted in the SDUSD, and continued indefinitely in the SDUSD at the grace of the court. Thereby, they would lose to the government another aspect of control concerning the health, welfare and education of their children, which could not have been anticipated by the parents who consented to compulsory education of their children in the neighborhood school system in effect when such laws were first passed in the early 1900s.

This trial judge pointed out in his Memorandum Decision filed March 9, 1978, that a substantial percentage of minority parents in the SDUSD, as well as majority parents, "object to 'busing' for various reasons," and that they had not had an opportunity to be heard in these proceedings. He added:

> "Further, there has been no showing of a violation of the United States Constitution. Under these circumstances, it is probable that such extensive mandatory measures would be impermissible under the Due Process Clause of the Fourteenth Amendment."

The compulsory education laws subject parents to fines and imprisonment if they fail to comply with mandatory busing assignments, under the requirement that every one of their children between the ages of 6 and 16 not exempted is subject to compulsory full-time education. See Education Code 48293.

The busing of unjoined interested children as sought by plaintiffs constitutes an arbitrary and unreasonable interference with the liberty of their unjoined interested parents by a defective process, in violation of the Due Process Clause.

21

VII

THE JUDICIAL ACTION SOUGHT BY PLAINTIFFS WOULD ABROGATE POWERS RESERVED TO THE PEOPLE AND OTHER CALIFORNIA GOVERNING AUTHORITIES, IN VIOLATION OF THE GUARANTEE CLAUSE OF THE CONSTITUTION

The drafters of the United States and California Constitutions sought to prevent the exercise of excessive governmental power by dividing it among three branches. One of the reasons for this division was so that the arm of government exercising force would not be sitting in judgment of its own action and there would be broad opportunities for peaceful and legal dissent and resort to the ballot.

Such governmental powers as have been delegated by the people of California have been divided among co-equal legislative, executive and judicial branches, and it is clear that their mandate is that none of the three branches is to assume power not granted to it.

The California Constitution provides in Article III, Sec. 3:

> "The powers of state government are legislative, executive, and judicial. Persons charged with the exercise of one power may not exercise either of the others except as permitted by this Constitution."

As the cases demonstrate, the California Supreme Court exercises the power of review to interpret the California Constitution. The right of the judiciary to exercise this power was enunciated by Chief Justice Marshall in Marbury v. Madison (1803), 5 U.S. (1 Cranch) 137. See also Bixby v. Pierno (1971), 4 Cal.3d 130 at 140.

Alexander Hamilton stated in Federalist No. 78 that if the

judges "should be disposed to exercise WILL instead of JUDGMENT the consequence would equally be the substitution of their pleasure to that of the legislative body." See Wright (editor), The Federalist (1961; Harvard Press), p. 493. Hamilton appeared confident that this would not happen because the judiciary "has no influence over either the sword or the purse; no direction either of the strength or of the wealth of the society; and can take no active resolution whatever. It may truly be said to have neither FORCE nor WILL, but merely judgment." Wright, supra, p. 490 (capital letters in original text). In the words of John Marshall: "Judicial power is never exercised for the purpose of giving effect to the will of the Judge; always for the purpose of giving effect to the will of the Legislature; or, in other words to the will of the law." Osborn v. Bank of the United States (1824), 22 U.S. 738 at 866.

That their judgment in reviewing legislation should be exercised by courts of last resort with great self-restraint is thoughtfully expounded by Justice Frankfurter in a concurring opinion in A. F. of L. v. American Sash Co.:

> "In the day-to-day work of our democracy it is vital that the power of the non-democratic organ of our Government be exercised with rigorous self-restraint... As history amply proves, the judiciary is prone to misconceive the public good by confounding private notions with constitutional requirements, and such misconceptions are not subject to legitimate displacement by the will of the people except at too slow a pace... (T)he Court is without power to shape measures for

23

dealing with the problems of society but has merely the power of negation over measures shaped by others..." 335 U.S. 538 at 555-557 (1949).

The admonishments of Marshall and Frankfurter apply with equal force to the California judiciary under the California Constitution, which vests the legislative power of the State in the California Legislature, which consists of the Senate and Assembly, "but the people reserve to themselves the powers of initiative and referendum." Article IV, Sec. 1, Cal. Const.

Californians have constitutionally provided for "a system of common schools by which a free school shall be kept up and supported in each district at least six months in every year..." They have granted the Legislature the power, by general law, to provide for "the incorporation and organization of school districts." Article IX, Secs. 5 and 14, Cal. Const.

The Legislature has enacted the Education Code, which provides the manner by which school districts are governed. Ed. Code, Secs. 35000 to 35351. The governing power of these school districts is vested in school board members elected by the qualified voters of the districts. See Ed. Code 35011. Also legislatively provided for is the means of support of the school districts, which includes taxes paid by the residents of the school districts. See Ed. Code, Secs. 42230-42247.

The electors of the SDUSD joined with others throughout California in enacting by initiative on November 7, 1972, Ed. Code 1009.6 (now Sec. 35351), which has never been repealed by the electors, to prohibit race discrimination in public school assignments.

24

The people of the SDUSD, through their representatives on the governing board, have adopted a voluntary integration plan.

The electors of the SDUSD joined with other California electors on November 6, 1979, in enacting legislatively-proposed Proposition 1 to amend their State Constitution.

Plaintiffs seek to have said plan superseded by a special master's plan which would (1) violate Ed. Code 35351 by mandating racially discriminatory busing of unjoined interested students; and (2) violate the California Constitution by mandating such busing for reasons not constitutionally sufficient under the U. S. Constitution.

Their only authority for the violation of the foregoing legislative and constitutional enactments of the people rests upon the series of California judicial rulings culminating in Crawford. A Supreme Court ruling in Santa Barbara Sch. Dist. v. Superior Court (1975), 13 Cal.3d 315, that Section 1009.6 "as applied to school districts manifesting either de jure or de facto segregation is unconstitutional" diminished the de jure-de facto distinction maintained by the Nation's highest court. Crawford then disregarded the distinction by holding that "racial segregation," as defined by the judging court, by itself, is the "evil" to be overcome by school districts under the California Constitution.

Thereby, the California high court dropped the necessity of showing de jure segregation in California school districts, without which the Swann Court said there would be no legal basis under the U. S. Constitution for busing.

But, because of Proposition 1, the California judiciary cannot

25

indirectly order busing solely upon a finding of de facto segregation. To do so would mean that the judicial branch of this State would be attempting to legislate their WILL concerning a particular sociological view as to the racial attendance to be maintained in the SDUSD. And to enforce such a busing edict would mean that the judiciary would be assuming the executive power of FORCE.

With remarkable prescience, Judge Learned Hand, in his 1958 Bill of Rights lectures at Harvard, warned of the effect of the assumption by the Supreme Court of the role of a third legislative chamber, which he indicated appeared then to be occurring in the school segregation cases. See Hand, The Bill of Rights (1958; Harvard Press) pp. 53-55.

Assuming, Hand said, that such a chamber with the power to annul statutes would be desirable, a suspensive veto did more than send back a challenged measure for renewed deliberation: "(I)t forbids it by making a different appraisal of the values, which...is the essence of legislation." And he stated that judges were seldom content merely to annul the particular solution before them, but usually wrapped up their veto in a protective veil of adjectives to imput to it a derivation "far more impressive than their personal preferences, which are all that in fact lie behind the decision." Hand, supra, pp. 68-70

Judge Hand pointed out the inexpediency of having judges serve as communal mentors and the increased likelihood of a resort to force in getting their commands obeyed, as personal notions of what they considered desirable were increasingly smuggled into decisions. He said it "does not accord with the underlying

26

presuppositions of popular government to vest in a chamber, unaccountable to anyone but itself, the power to suppress social experiments which it does not approve." Hand, supra, pp. 71-73.

A careful reading of the foregoing Frankfurter and Hand statements shows they saw no power in the federal judiciary to go beyond an occasional veto (exercised with restraint) of legislation to take affirmative action of a legislative nature. Yet, that is what plaintiffs ask the California judiciary to do in ordering busing for social purposes, in spite of similar "division of powers" provisions in the California Constitution.

Such action would usurp legislative and executive power constitutionally denied the State judiciary, and contravene Article IV, Sec. 4, of the United States Constitution, which provides in part: "The United States shall guarantee to every state in this Union a republican form of government..."

In determining whether this issue may here be considered, we turn first to <u>Luther</u> v. <u>Borden</u> (1849), 48 U.S. (7 Howard) 1, wherein two groups laid claims to recognition as to being the lawful government of Rhode Island. The Taney Court held that as to the claims in that case it was a political question beyond the appropriate sphere of action of the court properly belonging to Congress to decide as to the established government.

In <u>Highland Farms Dairy</u> v. <u>Agnew</u> (1937), 300 U.S. 608, it was held that a Virginia statute establishing a Milk Commission with power to create within the state natural market areas, and to fix the minimum and maximum prices to be charged for milk, was not a denial of a republican form of government. The Court went on to say that even if it were, the enforcement of that

27

guarantee, according to settled doctrine, is for the Congress, and not the courts.

Baker v. Carr, 369 U.S. 186, demonstrated in 1962 just how narrow the areas forbidden to the courts had become. In fact, numerous legal scholars have made the point that the Baker majority "never adequately answered...Frankfurter's argument that the equal protection claim it held to be justiciable was in effect a Guarantee Clause claim masquerading under a different label." See Berger, Government by Judiciary (1977); Harvard Press) at p. 80.

This case is readily distinguished from the foregoing cases in that plaintiffs are asking the State judiciary to exercise in a judicial proceeding legislative and executive powers these Interested Persons contend the Guarantee Clause will not permit it to use. Therefore, the Interested Persons against whom such powers are directed are entitled to raise legal objections in such proceedings to their use, which are peculiarly within the province of this Court to consider.

As stated in Serrano v. Priest (1976), 18 Cal.3d 728 at 764, the rulings of California courts are subject to the qualification that their interpretation may not restrict the guarantees according the national citizenry under the federal charter.

The awesome power which the exercise of WILL gives the judiciary is readily illustrated in comparing the problems faced by those challenging racial discrimination from a judicial source with the problems faced by those challenging such discrimination from other branches of government.

Those challenging racial discrimination against them from a judicial source face the disadvantage of being heard within

28

the same branch of government--the judiciary--whose authority they are challenging. The judiciary can also prevent their recourse to the ballot, as was done by declaring Ed. Code 1009.6 unconstitutional.

Peaceful boycott of discriminatory assignments by a school board under judicial compulsion makes boycotters subject to fines and imprisonment under compulsory attendance laws, prosecuted and enforced within the judicial branch. See Ed. Code 48293.

On the other hand, those challenging racial discrimination against them from legislative and/or executive sources, like Mrs. Rosa Parks and her associates, could, and did, engage in peaceful boycott against the Montgomery Bus Company; and could, and did, judicially question the constitutionality of discrimination against them under the Alabama laws to uphold their position. See Westin, The Trial of Martin Luther King (1974; Crowell Co.) pp. 25-27; also Browder v. Gayle, 142 F.Supp. 707; aff'd 352 U.S. 903 (1956).

The power derived from sitting in its own judgment becomes more awesome when one considers the FORCE available to the judiciary by contempt proceedings to carry out its WILL. The difference in challenging a state court judgment and challenging a state criminal statute, each by civil disobedience protesting state discriminatory actions, is drastic, as Dr. Martin Luther King found in disobeying an order prohibiting a march in Birmingham. Even if relief is sought from, and considered by, federal courts, judges give greater deference to court orders than to popular legislation. As a result, Dr. King was found in contempt and jailed for violation of a court order, even though that order

29

was based on a statute later found to be unconstitutional. Walker v. City of Birmingham (1966), 388 U.S. 307. His associate, Rev. Shuttlesworth, participated in the same march on April 12, 1963, but because he was charged with violating said unconstitutional statute--not a court order based on it--he was ultimately acquitted. Shuttlesworth v. Birmingham (1969), 394 U.S. 147.

Plaintiffs would have judicial WILL imposed indirectly upon the school board in San Diego to make racially discriminatory busing assignments adversely affecting Interested Persons, and judicial FORCE invoked to see that they are carried out. For this to occur on the record in this case would mean the accumulation of all governing powers in judicial hands. Such an abrogation of the prerogatives and powers of the people and the other branches of government in California is not permitted by the Guarantee Clause of our Constitution--the greatest instrument ever struck by a nation.

30

CONCLUSION

Plaintiffs' proposal, put simply, is that a special master, answerable only to the Court, shall mandatorily assign pupils so that every class in every district school shall have the racial balance he or she deems necessary to make them "integrated."

The rationale for this, to paraphrase Supreme Court Justice Rehnquist's statement in his September 12, 1980, order in Board of Ed., Los Angeles v. Superior Court, seems to be that "white" students, like text books, visual aids, and the like, are an element that every good school (and classroom therein) should have.

The results of carrying out of such a proposal--"white flight," decreased parental control over their child's education, decreased student privacy, decreased support for public schools, increased expense and use of fuel, environmental harm, and so forth--are all to be deemed irrelevant. And the objections to this method of integration--be they from educators, parents, students, electors, taxpayers or environmentalists--are all to be ignored as outside the issues between these two parties.

Justice Rehnquist, in the above order, indicated that the courts, sooner or later, will have to confront issues like "white flight" arising from such an approach. Fortunately, this Court has done that to a greater degree than any other court, attested to by this district's enviable position as the sole remaining large school district in the country not yet racially "imbalanced." In addition, this Court has recognized the legitimate objections of the parents of all races to forcible racial busing, to the extent it has been able to do so in their absence as parties.

The Court should continue to reject proposals, however sophisticated, to use its power to mandate racially discriminatory pupil assignments in the San Diego Unified School District.

DATED: October 10, 1980

Respectfully submitted,

Elmer Enstrom, Jr.

ELMER ENSTROM, JR., ESQ.
Attorney, in pro bono publico,
for Applicants-Movants
Groundswell, Larry K. Lester,
Stephen E. Lester, and
Christina Marie Lester,
as Interested Persons
and as Amici Curiae

32

SECTION 7(a), ARTICLE I, CALIFORNIA CONSTITUTION, AS AMENDED NOVEMBER 6, 1979 (PROPOSITION I)

Text of Proposed Law

This amendment proposed by Senate Constitutional Amendment No. 2 (Statutes of 1979, Resolution Chapter 18) expressly amends an existing section of the Constitution; therefore, new provisions proposed to be inserted or added are printed in *italic type* to indicate that they are new.

PROPOSED AMENDMENT TO ARTICLE I

Subdivision (a) of Section 7 is amended to read:

(a) A person may not be deprived of life, liberty, or property without due process of law or denied equal protection of the laws; *provided, that nothing contained herein or elsewhere in this Constitution imposes upon the State of California or any public entity, board, or official any obligations or responsibilities which exceed those imposed by the Equal Protection Clause of the 14th Amendment to the United States Constitution with respect to the use of pupil school assignment or pupil transportation. In enforcing this subdivision or any other provision of this Constitution, no court of this state may impose upon the State of California or any public entity, board, or official any obligation or responsibility with respect to the use of pupil school assignment or pupil transportation, (1) except to remedy a specific violation by such party that would also constitute a violation of the Equal Protection Clause of the 14th Amendment to the United States Constitution, and (2) unless a federal court would be permitted under federal decisional law to impose that obligation or responsibility upon such party to remedy the specific violation of the Equal Protection Clause of the 14th Amendment of the United States Constitution.*

Except as may be precluded by the Constitution of the United States, every existing judgment, decree, writ, or other order of a court of this state, whenever rendered, which includes provisions regarding pupil school assignment or pupil transportation, or which requires a plan including any such provisions shall, upon application to a court having jurisdiction by any interested person, be modified to conform to the provisions of this subdivision as amended, as applied to the facts which exist at the time of such modification.

In all actions or proceedings arising under or seeking application of the amendments to this subdivision proposed by the Legislature at its 1979–80 Regular Session, all courts, wherein such actions or proceedings are or may hereafter be pending, shall give such actions or proceedings first precedence over all other civil actions therein.

Nothing herein shall prohibit the governing board of a school district from voluntarily continuing or commencing a school integration plan after the effective date of this subdivision as amended.

In amending this subdivision, the Legislature and people of the State of California find and declare that this amendment is necessary to serve compelling public interests, including those of making the most effective use of the limited financial resources now and prospectively available to support public education, maximizing the educational opportunities and protecting the health and safety of all public school pupils, enhancing the ability of parents to participate in the educational process, preserving harmony and tranquility in this state and its public schools, preventing the waste of scarce fuel resources, and protecting the environment.

Appendix

CASE INDEX

(*Also see* Case Index in *Liberate Public Schools*, for cases cited in *Liberate Public Schools* and *Busing—Not Integration—Opposed*)

INDEX OF SUPREME COURT JUSTICES

(*Also see* Justices' Index in *Liberate Public Schools*, for justices referred to in *Liberate Public Schools* and *Busing—Opposed*)

**Judge, United States Court of Appeals, Second Circuit*

SUBJECT INDEX

(*Also see* Subject Index in *Liberate Public Schools*, for subjects referred to in *Liberate Public Schools* and *Busing—Opposed*)